CONFESSIONS OF A PROCESS JUNKIE
ILLUSTRATION TECHNIQUES FOR ADOBE ILLUSTRATOR

written, designed and edited by Alberto Ruiz.

printed in china
First edition, March 2007

ISBN 0-9793447-6-X

www.brandstudiopress.com

published by
brandstudio press
222-19 39th avenue
bayside, NY 11361
info@brandstudio.com

features

inking and coloring your sketches
adobe illustrator™

The approach described in the following steps has very little in common with techniques used in photo editing programs such as Adobe Photoshop or Painter, which manipulate pixels to achive the end result, instead you will be outlining and coloring simultaneously by tracing over your sketch and by overlapping vector shapes.

PREPARING AND SCANNING YOUR SKETCH

Since you would be basically tracing over your own sketch, using more than just the Pen tool, It helps tremendously to have a very clear image to go by. Think of it as drawing on top of a light box, you'd need a lot of guess work to trace over a fuzzy, cluttered sketch.

"Clean up" your drawing as much as possible before scanning, by erasing unwanted lines, excessive shading and smudging. Although your lines don't need to be perfect by any stretch, the closer your sketch resembles the final image the better.

A low resolution scan (anywhere from 72 to 150 dpi) is pretty much all you need to use as a template in Adobe Illustrator, a high-res image would only slow things down to a crawl.

I scanned this image at 100 dpi, to allow for zooming in very close on heavily detailed areas such as the gun, I then saved the scan in TIFF format (you can also place other file formats in Adobe Illustrator but TIFF, JPG and GIF files are preferred because of their small size).

If your drawing lines are still not sharp after scanning, open the sketch in Adobe Photoshop and play with the Levels slider, Command+L (Mac OS) Ctrl+L (Windows) to adjust the image to an acceptable clarity.

PLACING YOUR SCANNED IMAGE IN IILLUSTRATOR

After creating a new document in Illustrator, choose File > Place, a dialog box will prompt you to select a file to place, for this demonstration I chose draw_girl.tif from my desktop. Check the template box and click the Place button.

By the way, I work on a Mac so my screen and dialog boxes look different than the ones on a PC, the process is the same though.

By selecting the Template option, Illustrator dims the placed image by 50% (the default value, you can change the opacity level by double-clicking on the layer's name) this helps you see the lines and shapes you're creating as you ink or trace over the sketch. You can also resize, skew, flip or rotate the template at will after you unlock its layer (padlock icon on the layer palette). Illustrator also locks the Template layer and generates a new one *(Layer 1)* right above the template. **2**

PLANNING YOUR LAYERS

Managing a complex illustration is made easier by nesting groups of objects into layers, you should create as many layers as you deem necessary not just to organize but also to simplify the tedious process.

You can lock and hide layers to isolate and protect its contents or to avoid the obvious cluttering.

To further prevent or minimize the guess work and confusion on the work in progress, I identified and defined the various areas in my image before I started inking, by grouping elements in the image based on their overlapping order, and creating individual layers for each group.

Because of its complexity, I divided the hair into two groups, the shapes behind the girl's face became layer 1 (I double-clicked on its name to rename it *"Hair Back"*). Next, I created a second layer by clicking on the Create New Layer folded page icon located on the layer's palette (bottom row) I renamed it *"Girl's Face"*, followed by the hair overlapping the girl's face in it's own *"Hair Front"* group (layer3).

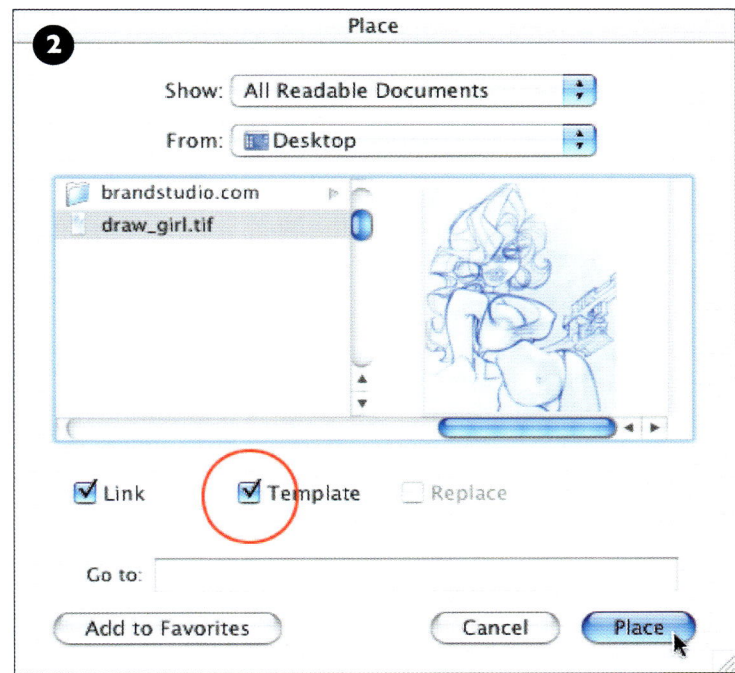

List of layers created for this image, in overlapping order from back to front:

1- *Hair Back*
2- *Girl's Face*
3- *Hair Front*
4- *Left Arm*
5- *Right Arm*
6- *Torso/Legs*

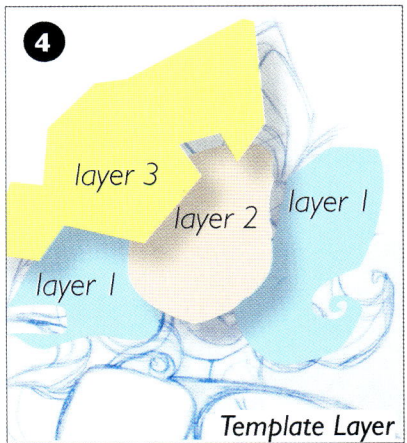

Graphical representation of the layering process.

SPLITTING THE HAIR

5 I started by tracing the contour of the hair behind the girl's face as one global shape with the Pen tool, using a 0.25 point black Stroke (outline) and no Fill, matching the lines of my sketch as close as possible.

The intersecting lines that make up the mosaic-like pattern inside the hair were drawn individually, using the same Stroke and Fill properties as the big shape. In order to apply the Divide Pathfinder filter effectively all the lines were drawn past the main hair shape's perimeter **6** I then grouped them together *Command+G (Mac OS) Ctrl+G (Windows)* and set the group's atributes to no Stroke and no Fill.

I selected all the elements I had drawn up to this point (including the main hair shape) by coosing Select > All from the top menu bar and clicked on the Divide Filter from the Pathfinder palette. **7** After the filter was applied, I deleted the residual shapes and proceeded to color the various objects.

Main hair shape path.

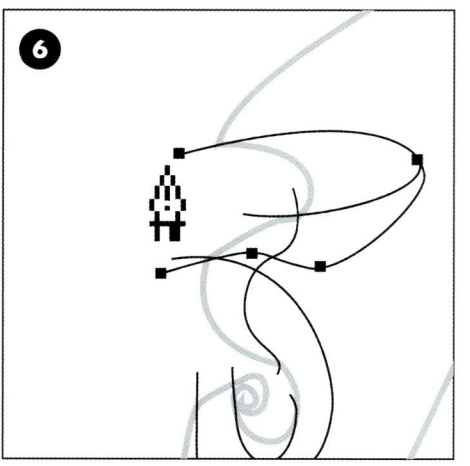

Intersecting lines past the main shape.

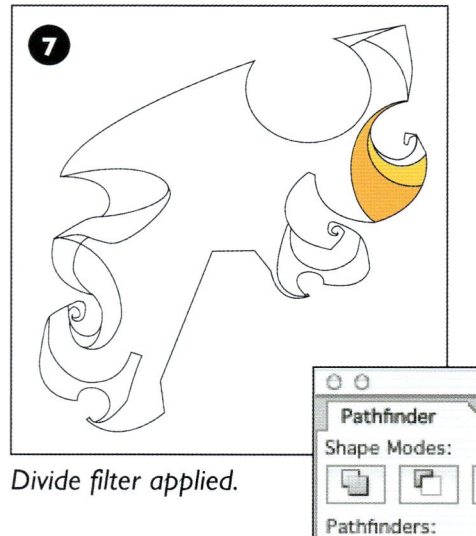

Divide filter applied.

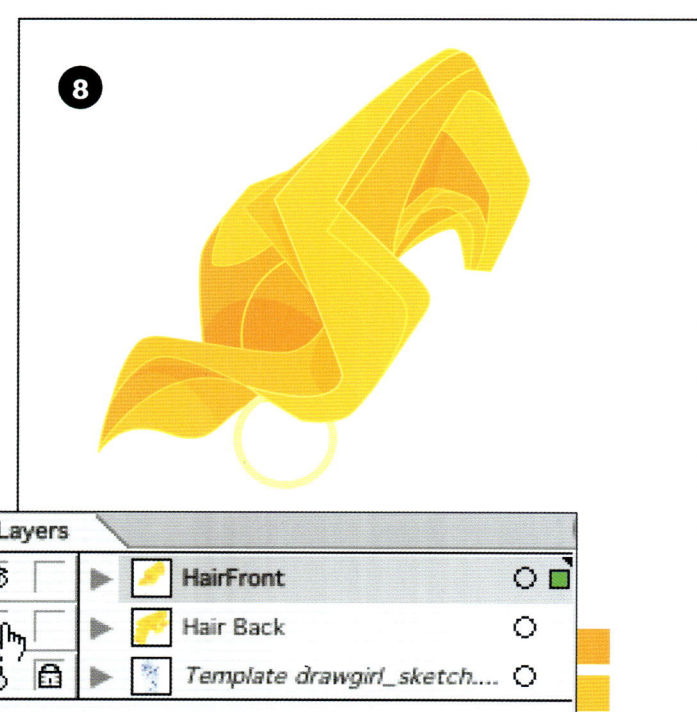

"Back Hair" layer hidden

Both layers visible

After finishing both hair groups, I got them out of the way by hiding them from view, this was accomplished by merely clicking on the eye icon in the Layers palette. Hold down Option/Alt as you click on the eye icon to show/hide all layers but the active one.

FACE VALUES

Before I started tracing the contour of the head, I created and named a new layer for the face, then I clicked and dragged the new layer and "sandwiched" it between layers 1 and 3 (the "Hair" layers). I set my object's atributes to No Fill from the icon at the bottom of the toolbox and mixed a medium flesh tone for the Stroke.

Zooming in at 300%, I drew a quick outline of the face using the pen tool. I kept the flesh colored Stroke without a Fill to be able to see the pencil outlines I was tracing over; I always get very excited at this point in the image, because faces are my favorite things to draw.

I began to lay down the rest of the objects in the face, as always working from back to front, I completed this part of the illustration in a very short amount of time, mostly because I don't have to be too careful about drawing parts of the image that will eventually be covered by overlapping objects,

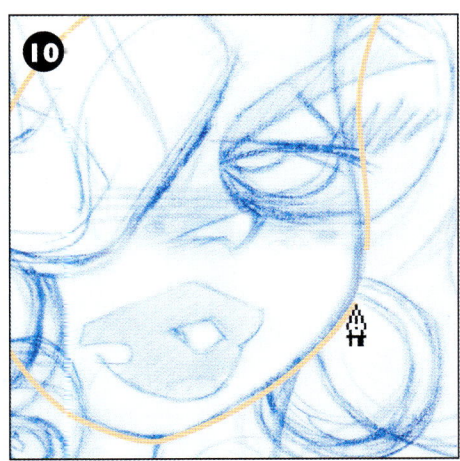
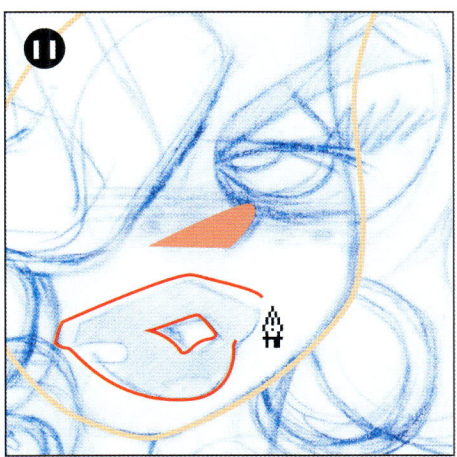
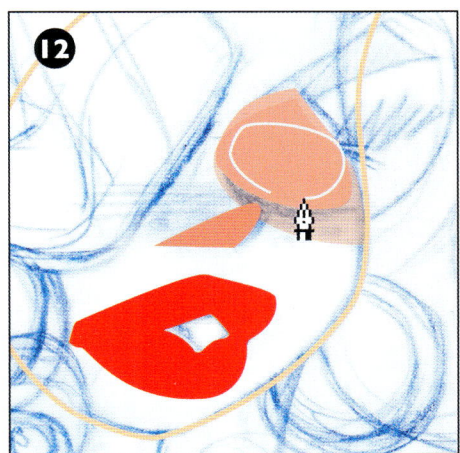

I skewed and rotated ellipses for most of the elements in the eye, as well as the shape of the nose.

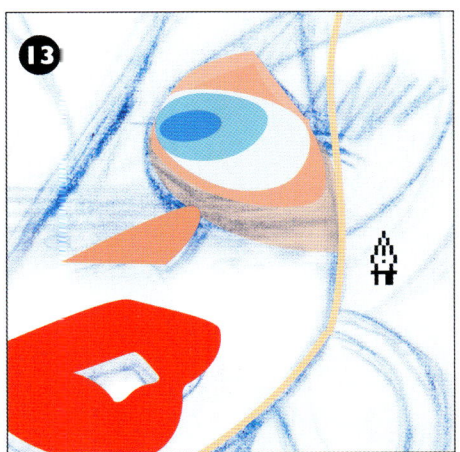
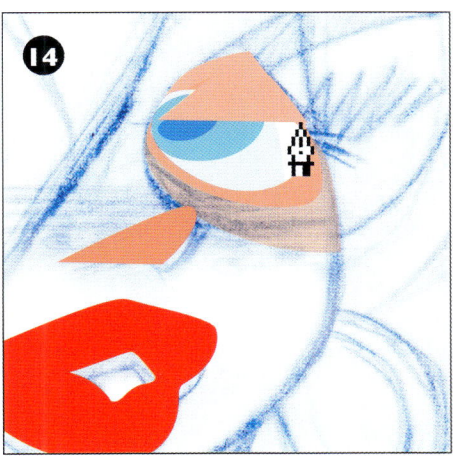
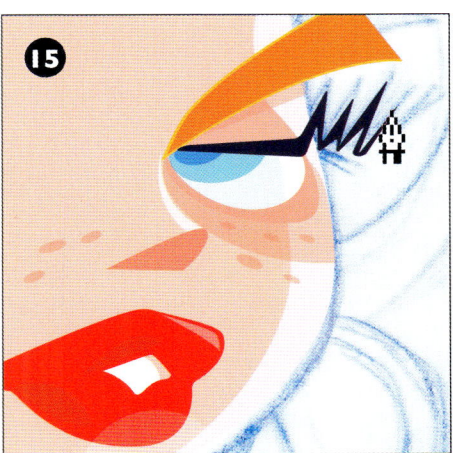

After most of the objects in the face were drawn, I held down *Command (Mac OS) Ctrl (Windows)* and clicked on the face outline to select it and switched the Stroke to Fill by clicking on the two-headed arched arrow (located between the Fill and Stroke icons at the bottom of the tool box) and began to add the high-lights and shadows.

FLESH TONES

I usually mix my colors as I go, I try to limit my palette to 3 shades of any one color: the object's main color, a darker shade for shadows and one for high-lights, this forces me to simplify the drawing and it also makes for more dramatic lighting.

Adobe Illustrator saves the current color palette you create within the document automatically, so if you mixed a set of flesh tones you really like in a previous file, you can import it at any time by choosing Window > Swatch Libraries > Other Library and selecting the file you wish to import a color palette from.

SOFT GRADIENTS

To complement the freckles and create a soft shadow, I placed 3 rectangles filled with the default black & white gradient from the Swatches palette at different angles, straight across the width of the face. 16

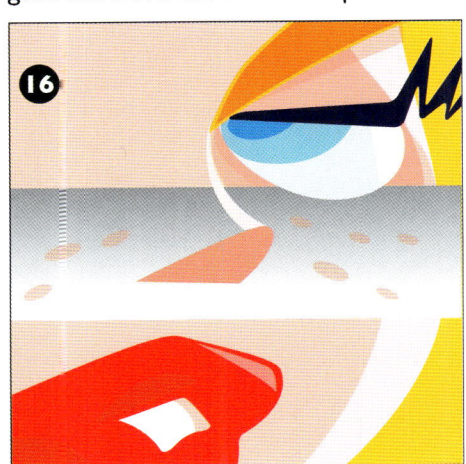

To achieve a smooth blend, In the Transparency palette I set the blend mode to Burn and the Opacity to 80%. 17

Bear in mind that this only works in RGB mode. In CMYK space you'd need to craeate a custom gradient.

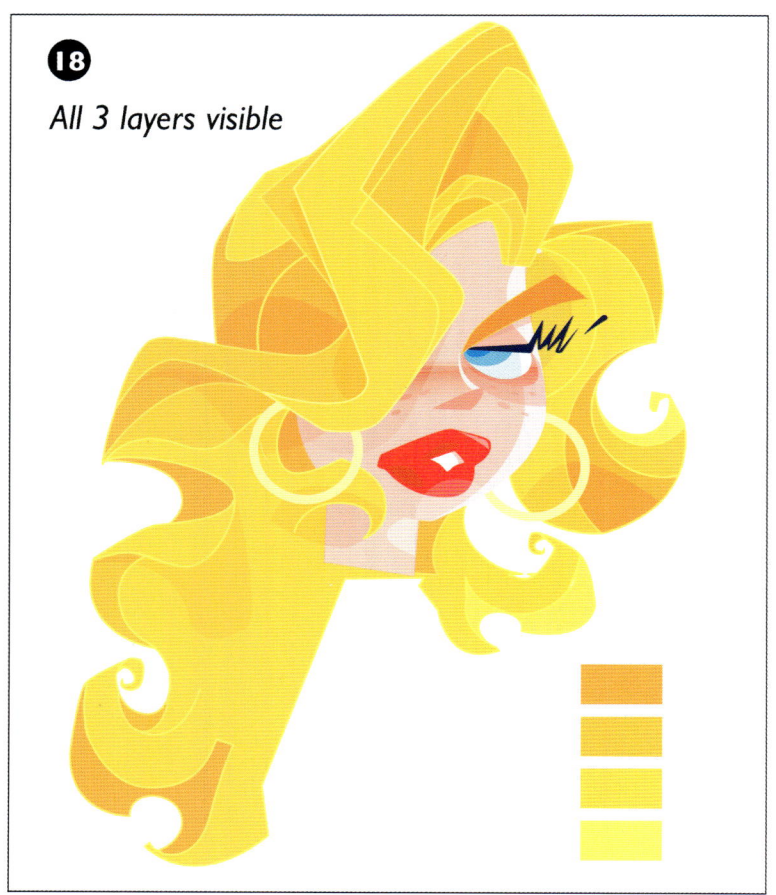

18

All 3 layers visible

TORSO, HIPS, ARMS AND FIREARMS

The torso and both arms were put together on separate layers, using the methods described earlier. Main shapes got divided to generate high-lights. Outlines were drawn mostly to keep same color shapes apart.

The right hand was added after the illustration was finished, the original sketch shows the girl leaning on a vehicle, her hand barely visible.

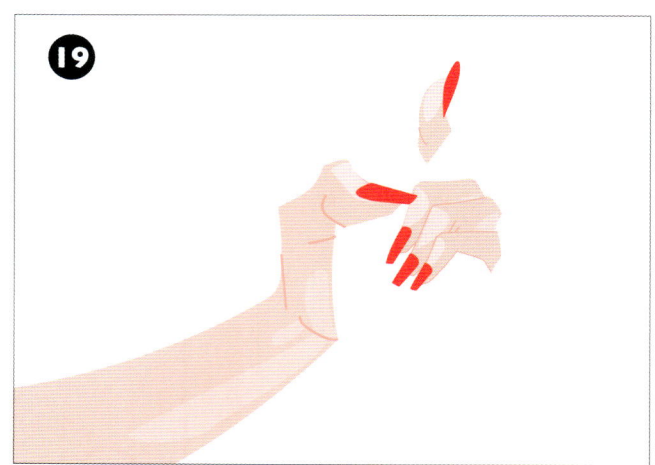

19

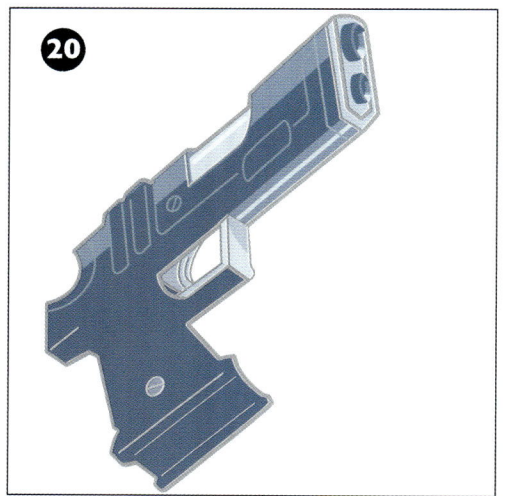

20

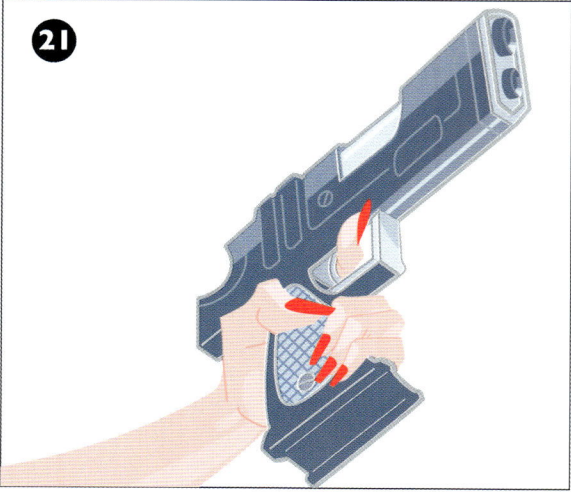

21

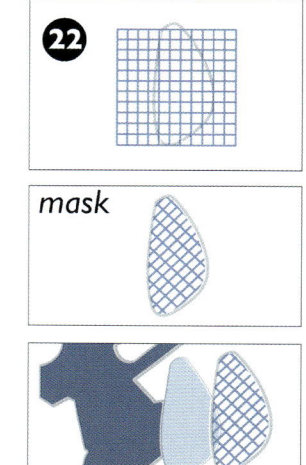

22

mask

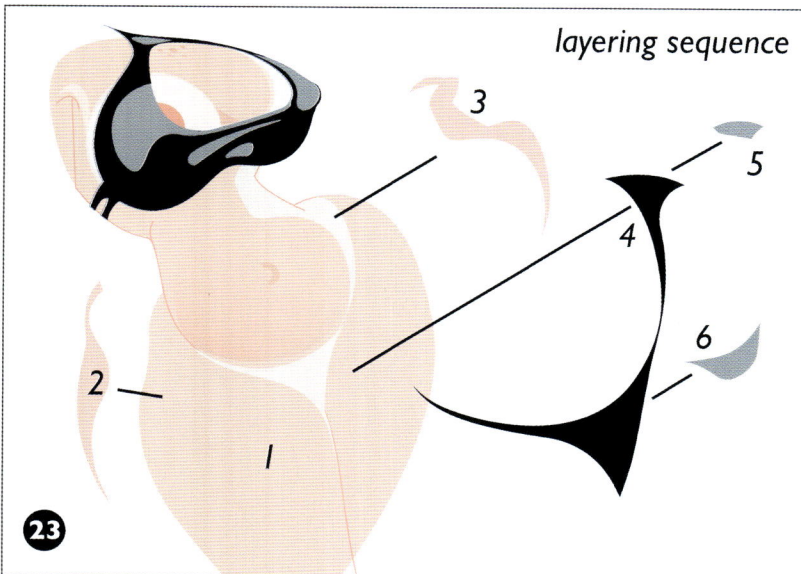

layering sequence

3

5

4

2

1

6

23

A SIMPLE MASK

I created the mesh for the gun handle easily by selecting the Rectangular Grid tool and clicking and dragging across the screen. To specify the amount of horizontal and vertical dividers beforehand, click once on the screen while having the tool selected.

 I skewed the grid to my liking with the aid of the Shear tool and masked the grid into the elipse by selecting both the grid and the shape and choosing *Object > Clipping Mask > Make* from the top menu bar, you can also use *Command+7 (Mac OS) Ctrl+7 (Windows)* Make sure that the shape is always in front of the object (s) you wish to mask. **22**

working with transparency blends
adobe illustrator™

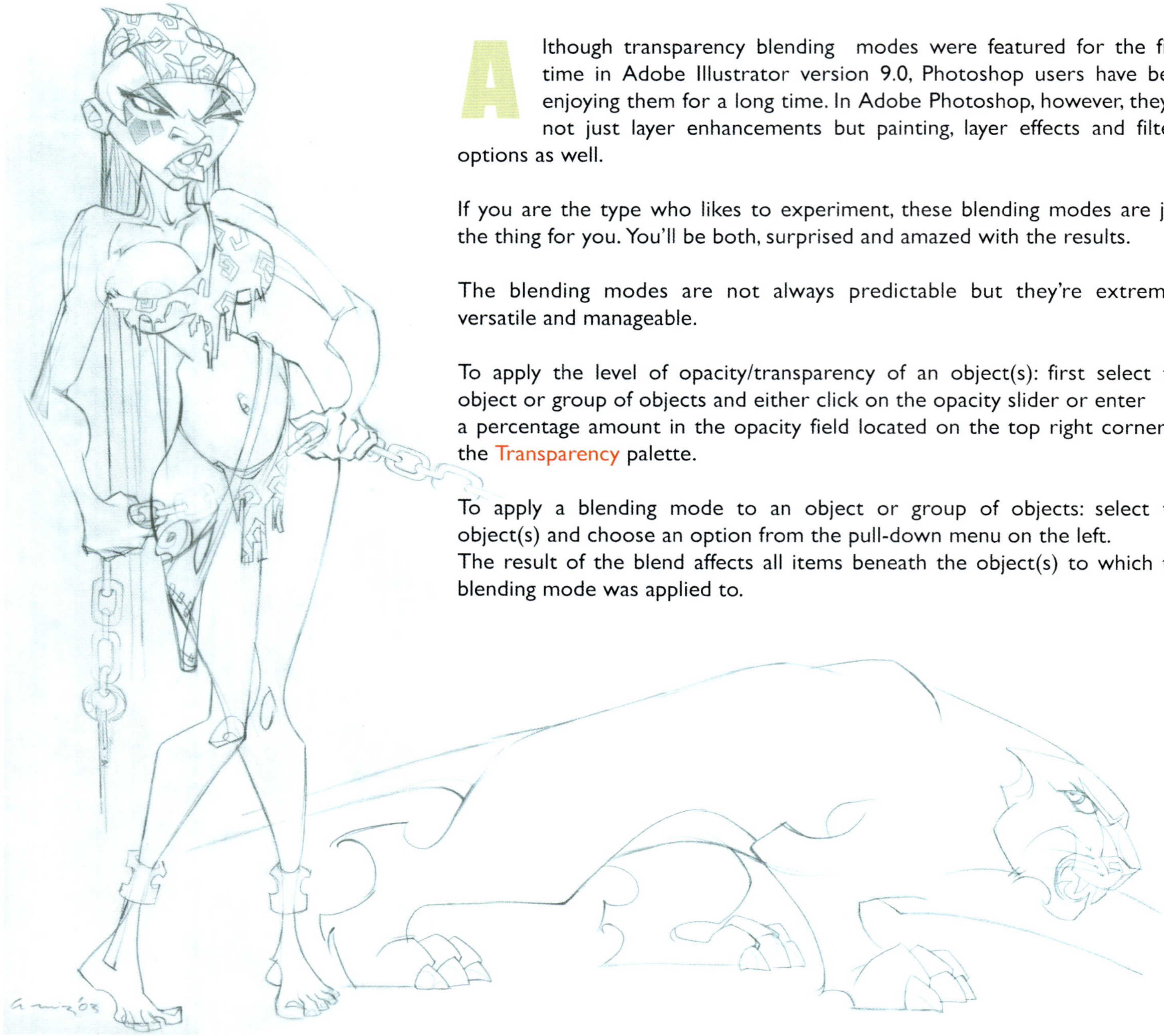

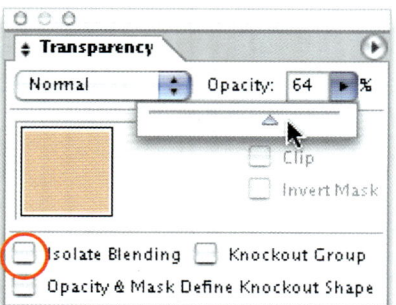

Although transparency blending modes were featured for the first time in Adobe Illustrator version 9.0, Photoshop users have been enjoying them for a long time. In Adobe Photoshop, however, they're not just layer enhancements but painting, layer effects and filter's options as well.

If you are the type who likes to experiment, these blending modes are just the thing for you. You'll be both, surprised and amazed with the results.

The blending modes are not always predictable but they're extremely versatile and manageable.

To apply the level of opacity/transparency of an object(s): first select the object or group of objects and either click on the opacity slider or enter a percentage amount in the opacity field located on the top right corner of the Transparency palette.

To apply a blending mode to an object or group of objects: select the object(s) and choose an option from the pull-down menu on the left. The result of the blend affects all items beneath the object(s) to which the blending mode was applied to.

To confine the effects of the blending modes to only a group of objects: first select the group and click on the Isolate Blending check-box (red circle). Only the selected objects will be affected by the blending modes.

TRANSPARENCY PALETTE: CAUSE AND EFFECT

The following is an overview of the 4 blending modes used to color the illustration in this article and my personal approach to solving these design problems. In no way this can even begin to scratch the surface as far as the creative possibilities these blending modes offer. Go ahead and have fun.

SHADOWS AND HIGHLIGHTS FROM A SINGLE COLOR

An extensive color palette can be generated by overlapping two or more objects of the same color and applying the various modes at different levels of opacity. Blend with different colors to achieve richer shadows and highlights.

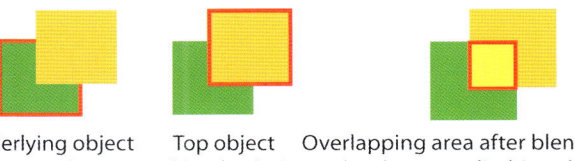

Underlying object (base color) | Top object (blend color). | Overlapping area after blending mode has been applied (result color)

SHADOWS

MULTIPLY: Multiplies the base color by the blend color until it reaches black.

C: 9
M: 34
Y: 31
K: 1

Same color multiplied against itself

100% opacity   100% opacity   50% opacity   25% opacity

blended with pink & lavender

100% opacity   100% opacity

C: 6
M: 46
Y: 0
K: 0

COLOR BURN: Darkens the base color to reflect the blend color by increasing the contrast.

C: 35
M: 30
Y: 0
K: 0

Same color blended against itself

100% opacity   100% opacity   50% opacity   25% opacity

blended with pink & lavender

100% opacity   100% opacity

HIGHLIGHTS

SCREEN: Lightens the base color by screening it against the blend color until it reaches white.

C: 9
M: 34
Y: 31
K: 1

Same color screened against itself

100% opacity   100% opacity   50% opacity   25% opacity

blended with yellow & orange

100% opacity   100% opacity

C: 4
M: 24
Y: 75
K: 1

COLOR DODGE: Increases the brightness of base color to reflect the blend color.

C: 35
M: 30
Y: 0
K: 0

Same color blended against itself

100% opacity   100% opacity   50% opacity   25% opacity

blended with yellow & orange

100% opacity   100% opacity

BLENDING MODES USED WITH GRADIENTS   MULTIPLE MODES / MULTIPLE SHAPES

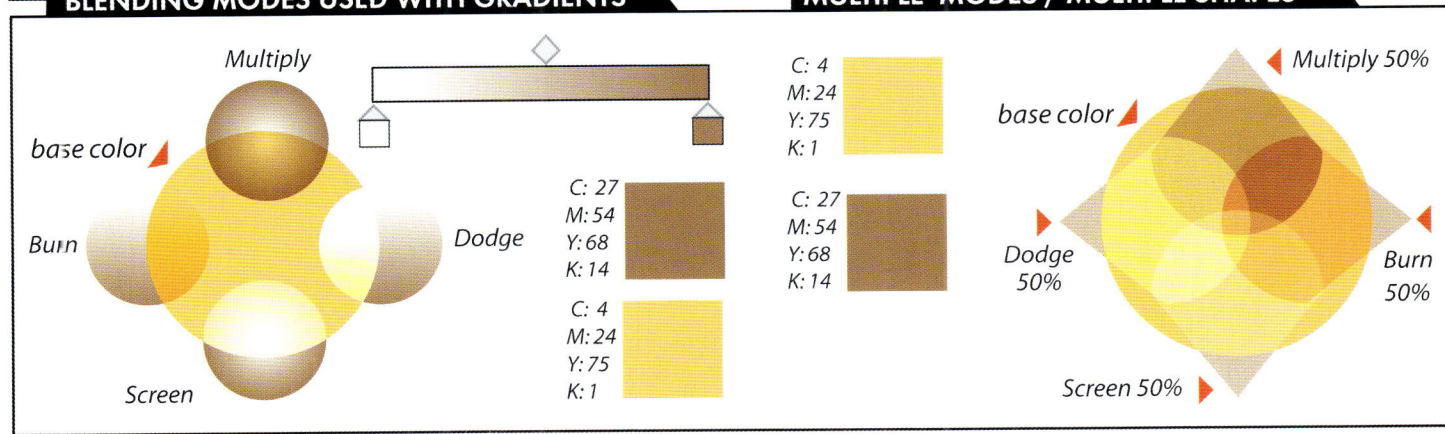

Multiply

base color

Burn   Dodge

Screen

C: 4
M: 24
Y: 75
K: 1

C: 27
M: 54
Y: 68
K: 14

C: 4
M: 24
Y: 75
K: 1

C: 27
M: 54
Y: 68
K: 14

Multiply 50%

base color

Dodge 50%   Burn 50%

Screen 50%

NO FONT, NO PROBLEM

Howard didn't remember what the name of the typeface he used for his comic was and I just didn't want to go through a quazillion fonts looking for the perfect match. Since I had scanned one of his covers, in grayscale as a bitmap TIF, all I did was to use the Auto Trace tool.

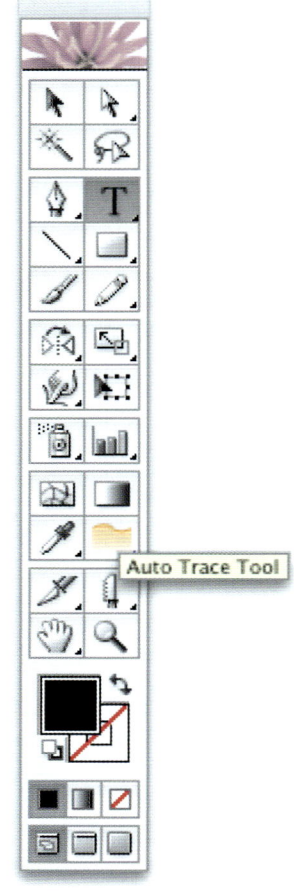

Original bitmap scan of the logo.

The Auto Trace tool is a snap to use, just click on the bitmap image you want to convert to vestor shapes and bingo! Of course, like anything digital, it doesn't work miracles, *"garbage in,garbage out"*. Make sure your scan is of a decent qualit, the sharper your image, the more accurate the conversion.

After the conversion I "cleaned" the logo, with the Pen tool. Sometimes you'd need to sharpen a corner here and there, luckily there wasn't much time spent fixing the resulting vector shapes of the logo, as the scan I used was of good resolution.

layering sequence starting from the foremost object to the furthest in the back.

In order to make the title "pop" against the busy and dark ground I made 4 copies of the logotype and filled one of them with a flat green, the transparency blend set to dodge the one underneath was filled with a lighter version of the repeat pattern I'd be using for the background itself, set to normal.

Finally, a thick "glowing " outline was attributed to the copy of the logo placed in front of the others and a dark green for the last copy sent all the way back.

The final logo may not look like much now but it will do the trick once I place it against a deep, dark green background.

C: 27
M: 54
Y: 68
K: 14

C: 4
M: 24
Y: 75
K: 1

C: 4
M: 24
Y: 75
K: 1

C: 27
M: 54
Y: 68
K: 14

C: 27
M: 54
Y: 68
K: 14

MINUS FRONT

The 'Exclude overlapping shape areas' tool, formerly known as Minus Front can be found in the Pathfinder palette. It does exactly what it says it does.

Draw elipse

Clone elipse & offset

Apply "Exclude" filter

STRAIGHT FACE

The objects —as they are called in Adobe Illustrator— that make up the face were drawn with the Pen tool, using mostly straight lines and jagged-edged shapes. They were colored using the blending modes "single color method" described on the previous page.

The general outline of the face was drawn first and the rest of the shapes were drawn "free hand" paying little or no attention to the original sketch. Many of these objects were cloned and piled up on top of one another at different blending modes to either darken or lighten a particular area, no sciense here, just trial and error.

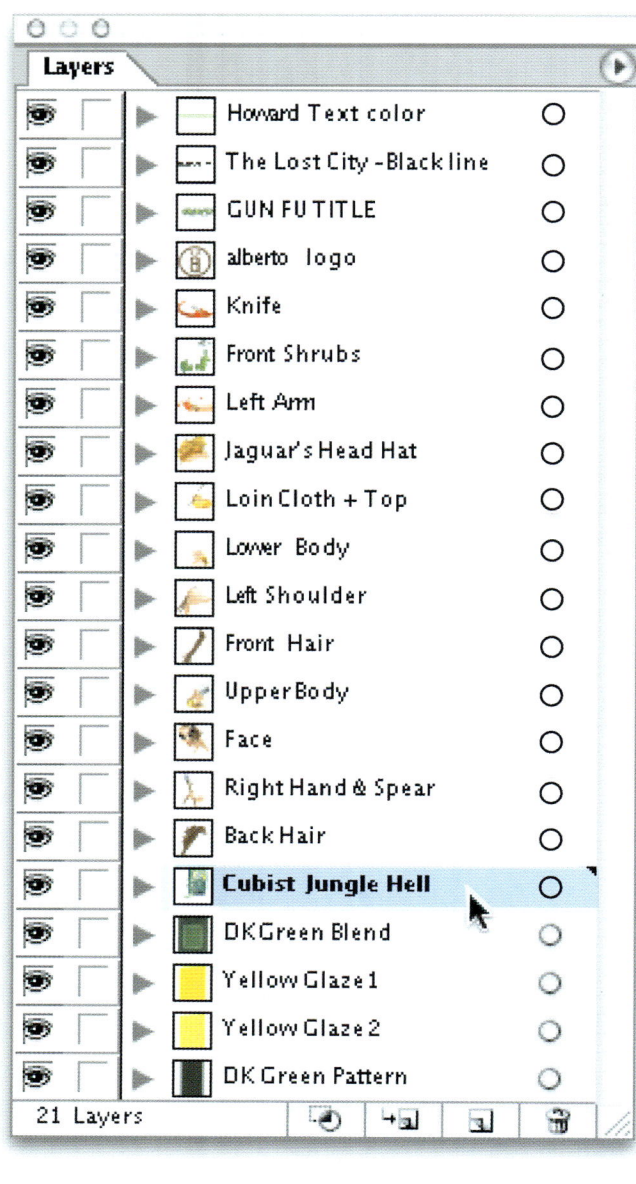

A LOGISTICAL NIGHTMARE

As with any complex illustration, collecting groups of related objects into layers really helps managing the file. The finished illustration contains in excess of 1800 individual objects, —there are 20 layers in this file.

HAIR TREATMENT

The hair was drawn just like the teacher told me to: in clumps. large shapes first and individual strands were thrown about for that "hair in motion" effect. I wouldn't draw every single strand in real life and I wouldn't dream of doing it in the computer either, so just like in real life drawing, a big chunk with a few strands to fool the eye is what you get..

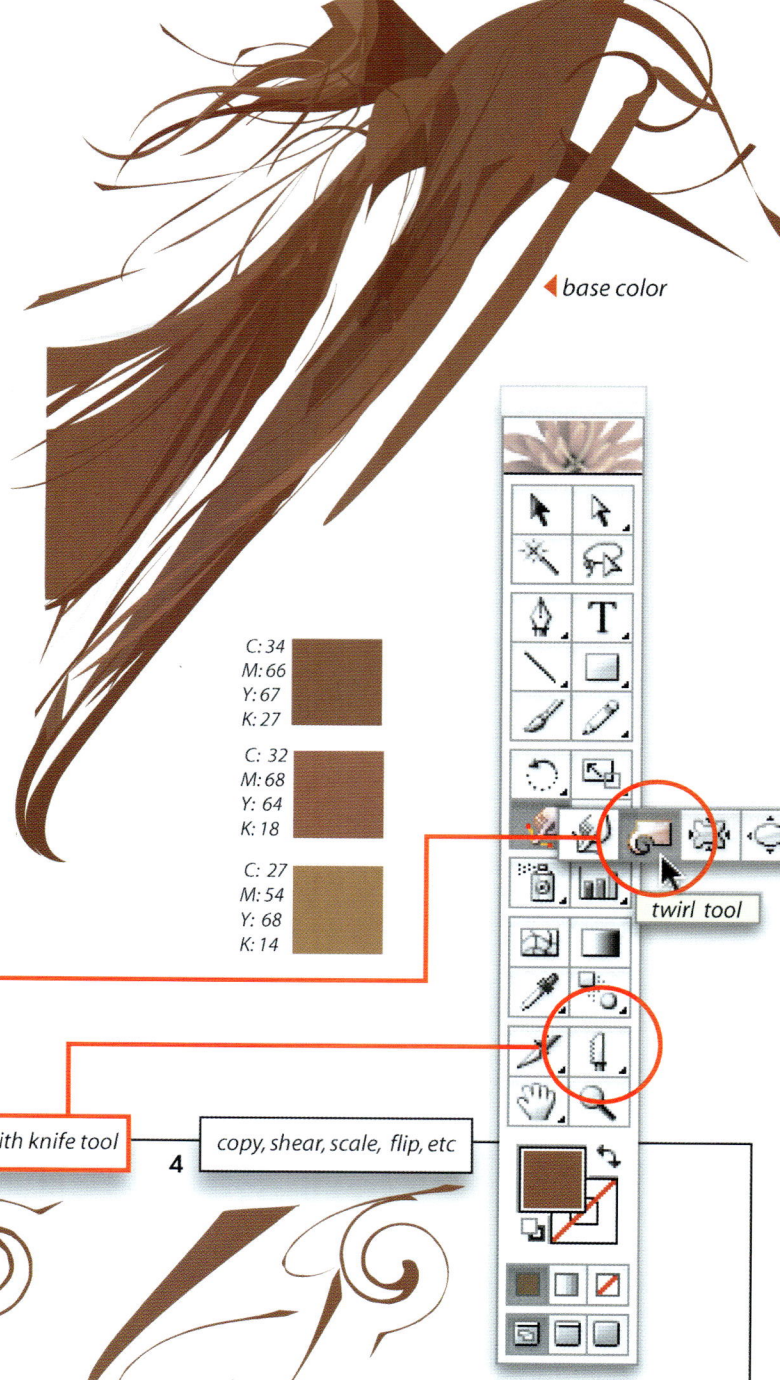

◄ base color

C: 34
M: 66
Y: 67
K: 27

C: 32
M: 68
Y: 64
K: 18

C: 27
M: 54
Y: 68
K: 14

twirl tool

Although the hair looks complicated, in reality only the big shapes were carefully drawn, just as in the jungle background one or two shapes were cloned endlessly by clicking and dragging while holding the option key *(Alt in Windows)* and modified to fill in the rest of the hair mass.

Transparency blend modes were applied to overlapping hair shapes as well.

| 1 | *draw a shape* | 2 | *twirl shapes* | 3 | *cut shapes with knife tool* | 4 | *copy, shear, scale, flip, etc* |

BRITNEY'S SPEAR THIS AIN'T

Nothing special about the spear's head coloring, with one exception: white colored shapes were sandwiched between objects with shades of blue at 62% percent opacity to provide edge highlights.
The spear's wooden handle was colored using 4 shapes of the same shade of brown, all set to multiply, and each of the objects was given a slightly incremental opacity value, using white as the base color.

Not unlike the other elements in the illustration, one or two shapes were tweaked and cloned to speed up the process in some instances the same shape was just slightly offset.

multiply 44% C: 60
M: 32
Y: 27
K: 3

multiply 43% C: 50
M: 24
Y: 8
K: 7

white
62%

C: 37
M: 24
Y: 8
K: 2

base color

C: 27
M: 54
Y: 68
K: 14

base color: white

24%   27%

34%   43%

multiply

HOME GROWN GRASS

One blade of grass
cloned & tweaked,
same as the hair.

base color ▶

multiply 44%
C: 74
M: 5
Y: 100
K: 0

Screen 85%
C: 74
M: 5
Y: 100
K: 0

A BACKGROUND WITHIN A BACKGROUND

I have an fascination with characters sticking out of frames, this is because as a kid I loved watching the cartoons in which characters would dive into and out of framed paintings or painted elaborate landscapes themselves to which only they had access. I imagined the characters jumping out of the TV right into my living room. The geometric jungle here is framed by the fake *"Mayan"* repeat, to help explain the geography. Although this pattern used to be part of the Illustrator package, I dissected it here for instructional purposes.

MAYAN REPEAT
1   2   *copy & paste*   3   *flip*   4   *color shapes*   5   *add green square*   6   *drag to swatches*

HOW TO PUNCH A HOLE THROUGH A WALL

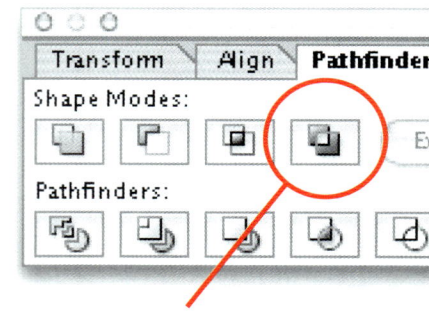

A   *Exclude overlapping shape areas (formerly known as "Minus Front")*

Draw a rectangle *(lt. green)*, now draw a smaller one in the center *(dk. green)*, select both shapes and from the Pathfinder palette click on the Exclude icon fig. A the end result is a compound object that retains the attributes of the top-most object, in this case the dk. green rectangle. Fill the shape with the *"Mayan"* repeat pattern from the Swatches palette. Voila!

multiple blending modes ▼

◄ *base color*

◄ *Multiply 50%*

◄ *Multiply 50%*

◄ *Screen 100%*

base color ►

FRAME SEQUENCE

To soften the intensity of the repeat pattern, I blended 2 copies of the frame with different shades of green at different opacity levels using the multiply and the screen blending mode options. I offset the cut out area to allow the pattern to show through without the dark green blend. The end result gave me a richer, darker background..

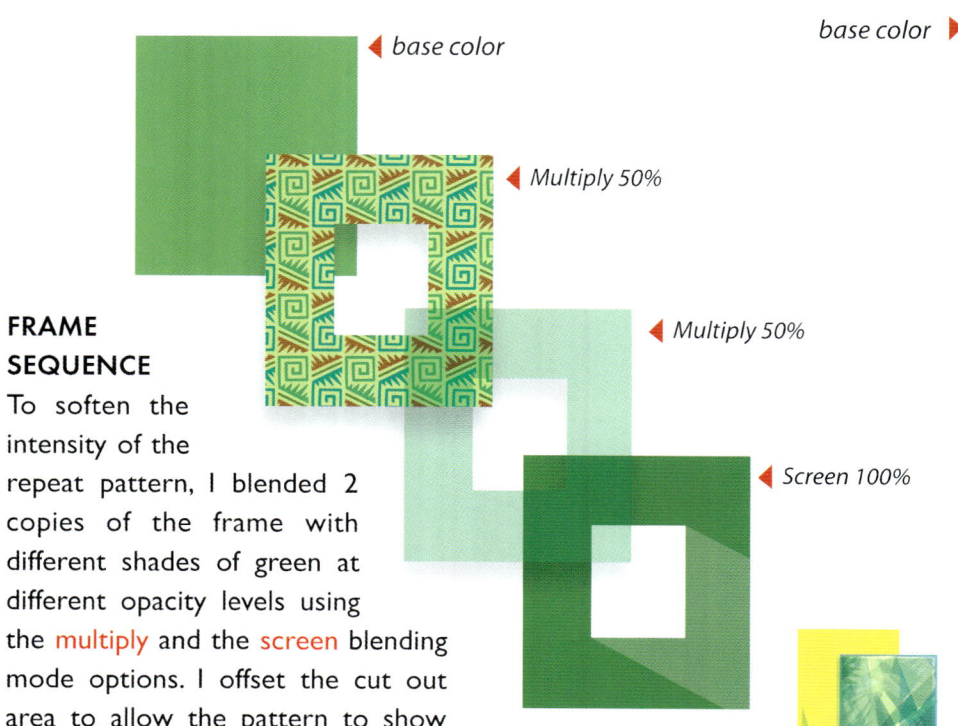

CUBIST JUNGLE HELL

I weaseled my way out of drawing an actual jungle by creating an assimetrical star-like shape and a couple of triangles, which I basically cloned repeatedly at various sizes, angles and transparency blend modes.

BITMAP TEXTURE FUN

HIGH SPEED CHASE

mporting photographic textures and effects to and add dimension and excitement to otherwise flat vector art is a lot of fun and it couldn't be easier. Adobe Illustrator lets you bring Photoshop generated bitmap images through its Place command, which can be transformed with a click of the mouse. In addition to textures, you also have the capability of placing inked drawings, black and white photographs and sketches for easy coloring and tinting. A bitmap file looks deceptively like a good old high-contrast, black and white image. Its magic, however, lies in its transparency properties, the *black* part of the bitmap is opaque and can be re-colored at will, while the apparent *white* area is actually 100 % transparent, allowing for a myriad of design possibilities.

HIGH SPEED COLORING JOB

I scanned the above inked drawing as "line art/text" at 600 DPI, and saved the image in TIF format. After creating a new document in AI I placed the file by choosing "Place" from the File menu. By the way, most high-resolution TIF bitmap files are under a megabyte in size.

NOTE: It's important that you keep all TIF files associated with the work you are doing in the same folder along with the main Illustrator document as AI keeps track of the linked files' location.

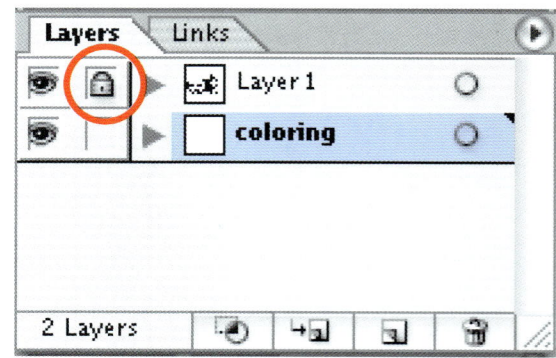

I locked the current layer *(Layer 1)* created a second layer which I re-named "coloring" and dragged directly underneath. You should also keep in mind that you can chage the default grayscale (black) bitmap to any custom, CMYK, RGB, or PMS color you wish but you can't fill the image with patterns or gradients.

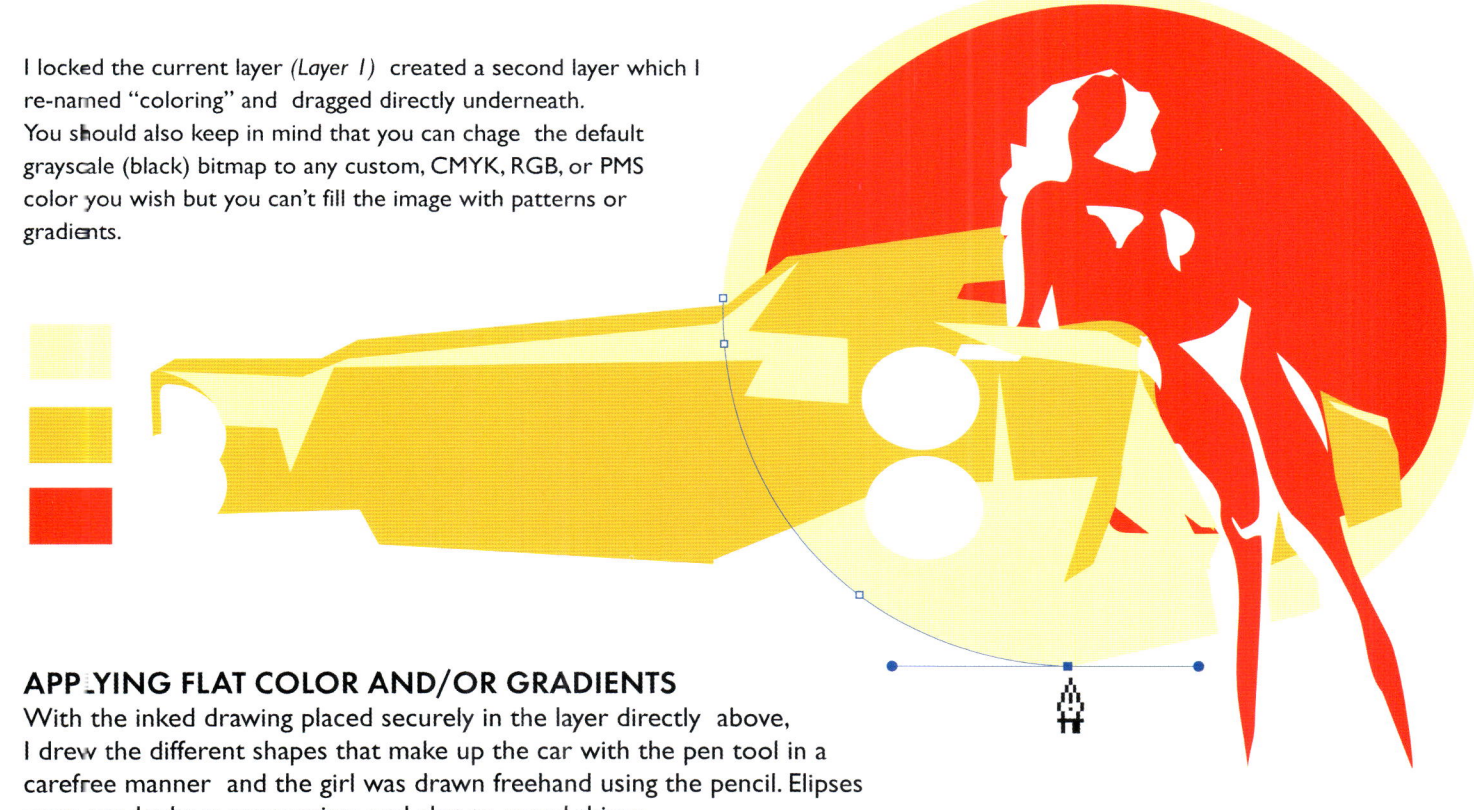

APPLYING FLAT COLOR AND/OR GRADIENTS

With the inked drawing placed securely in the layer directly above, I drew the different shapes that make up the car with the pen tool in a carefree manner and the girl was drawn freehand using the pencil. Elipses were used where appropriate and also to speed things.

FINAL ILLUSTRATION

For this particular piece I offset the colored shapes a bit, but you can color yours as tight or loose as you want, knowing the black line or layered colors will overlap and hide any inconsistencies.

COLORING A QUICK SKETCH

1 After scanning in Grayscale mode, the contrast was improved using the Levels slider in Adobe Photoshop—*Command+L (Mac OS) Ctrl+L (Windows)*— and the image was inverted —*Command+I (Mac OS) Ctrl+I (Windows)*— **2** The mode was converted from Grayscale to Bitmap using the Diffusion Dither Method at an output of 600 pixels per inch. **3**

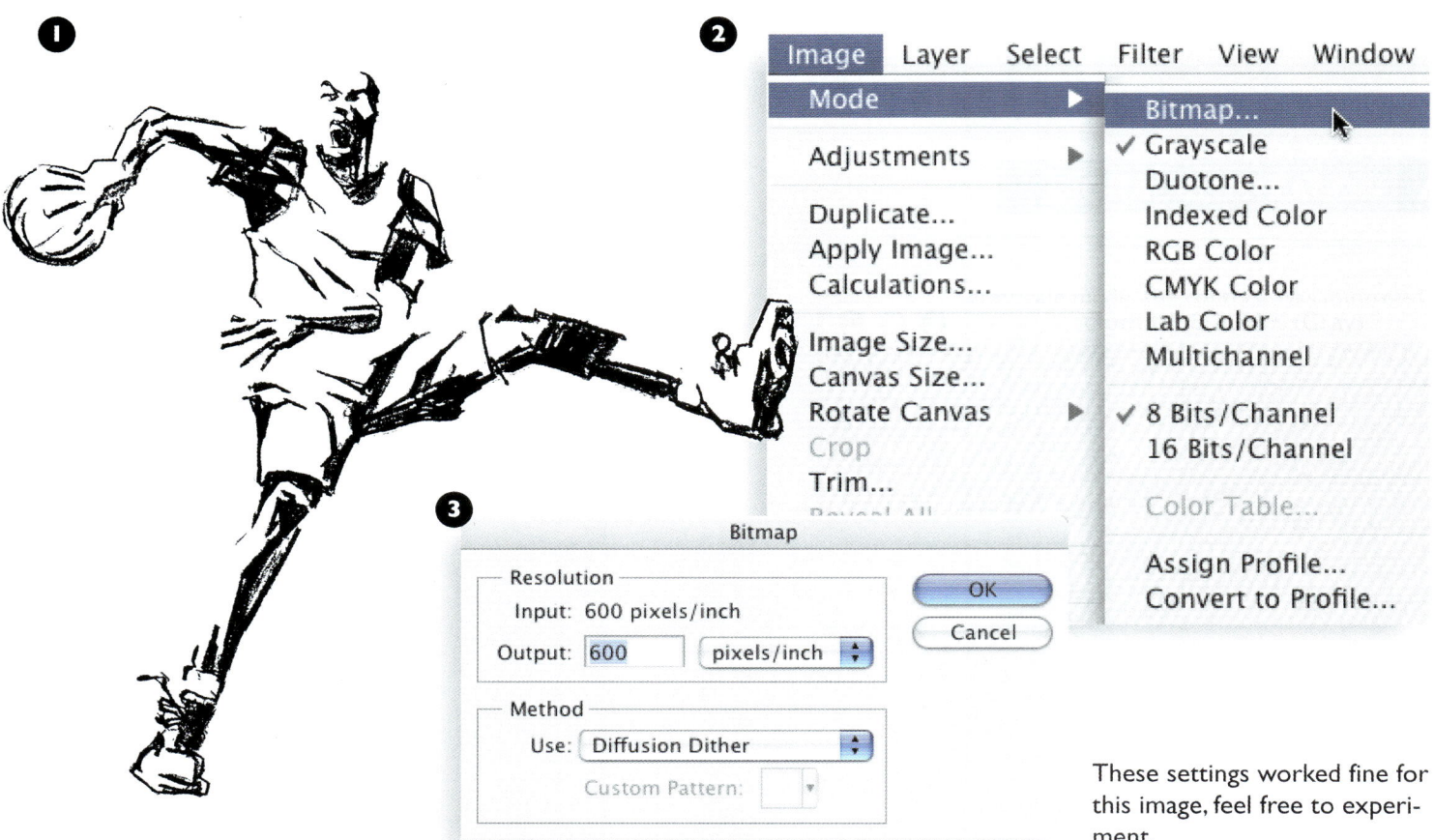

These settings worked fine for this image, feel free to experiment.

4 I added a chain-link fence, which I also inverted.

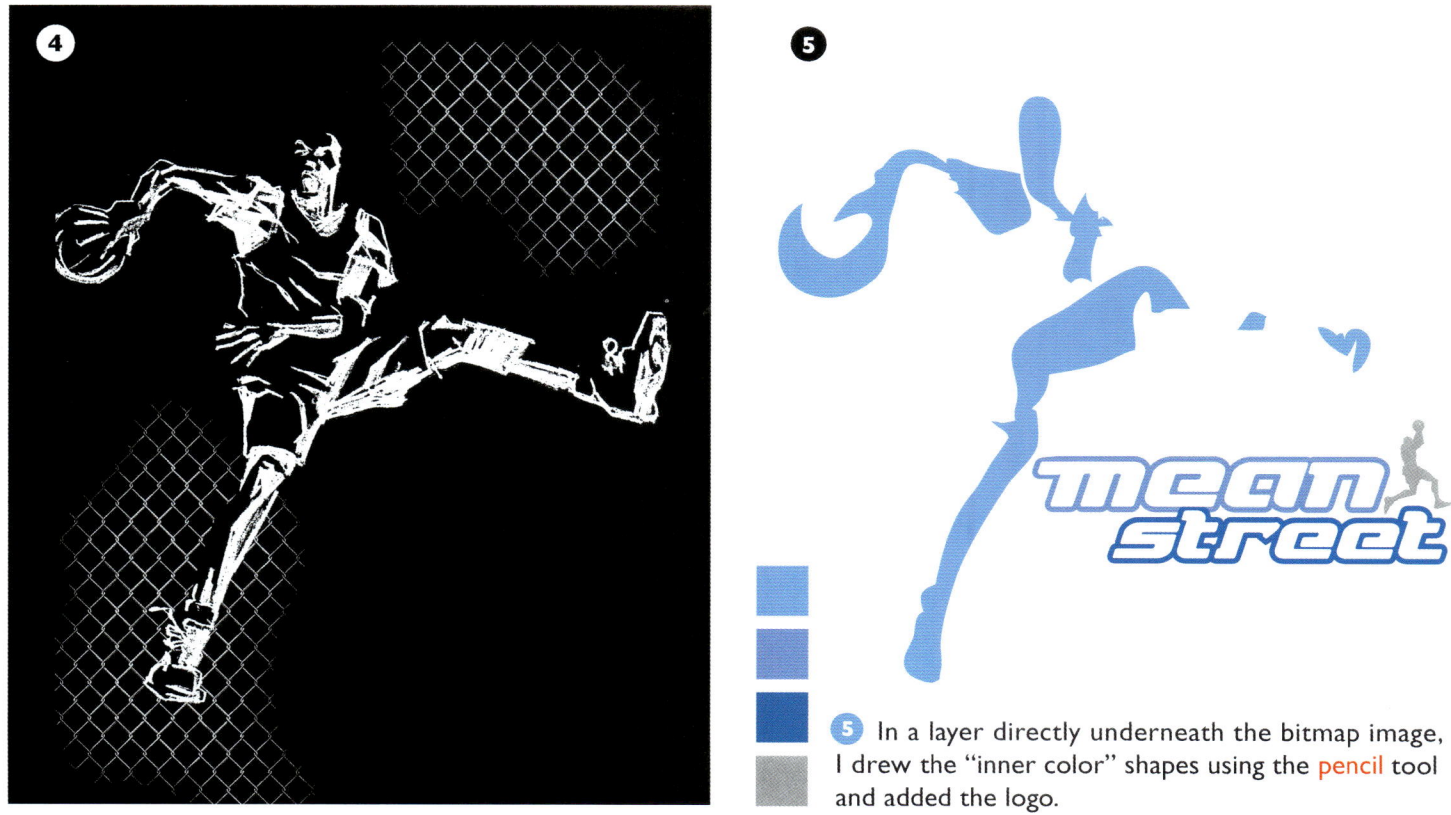

5 In a layer directly underneath the bitmap image, I drew the "inner color" shapes using the pencil tool and added the logo.

The basketball as a design element was an afterthought, I felt the figure needed more than ust a black background. The chain link fence was cut from the main picture and savec as a bitmap as well, several copies were colored red and scattered all over the ball for texture.

Transparency
Gradient
Overlay
Opacity: 60 %
Clip
Invert Mask

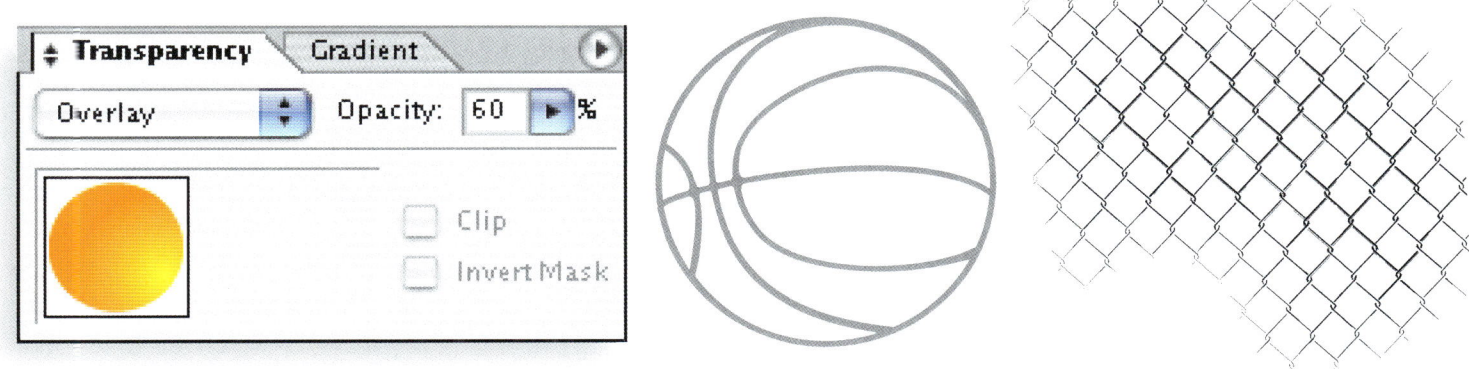

Three circles were placed behind the basketball. a. fill with a gradient and b. filled with dots, both set at 60% Overlay

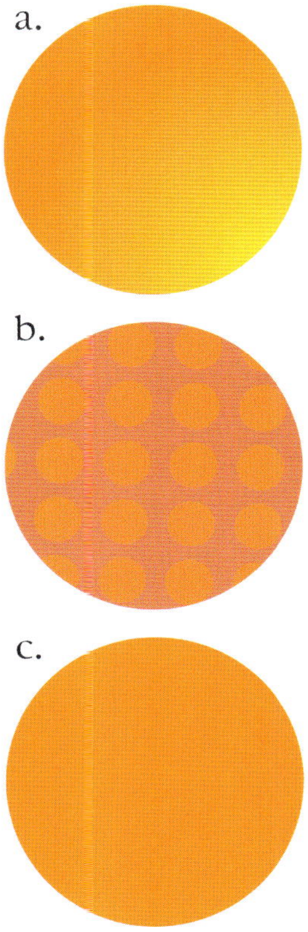

a.
b.
c.

Layering order.

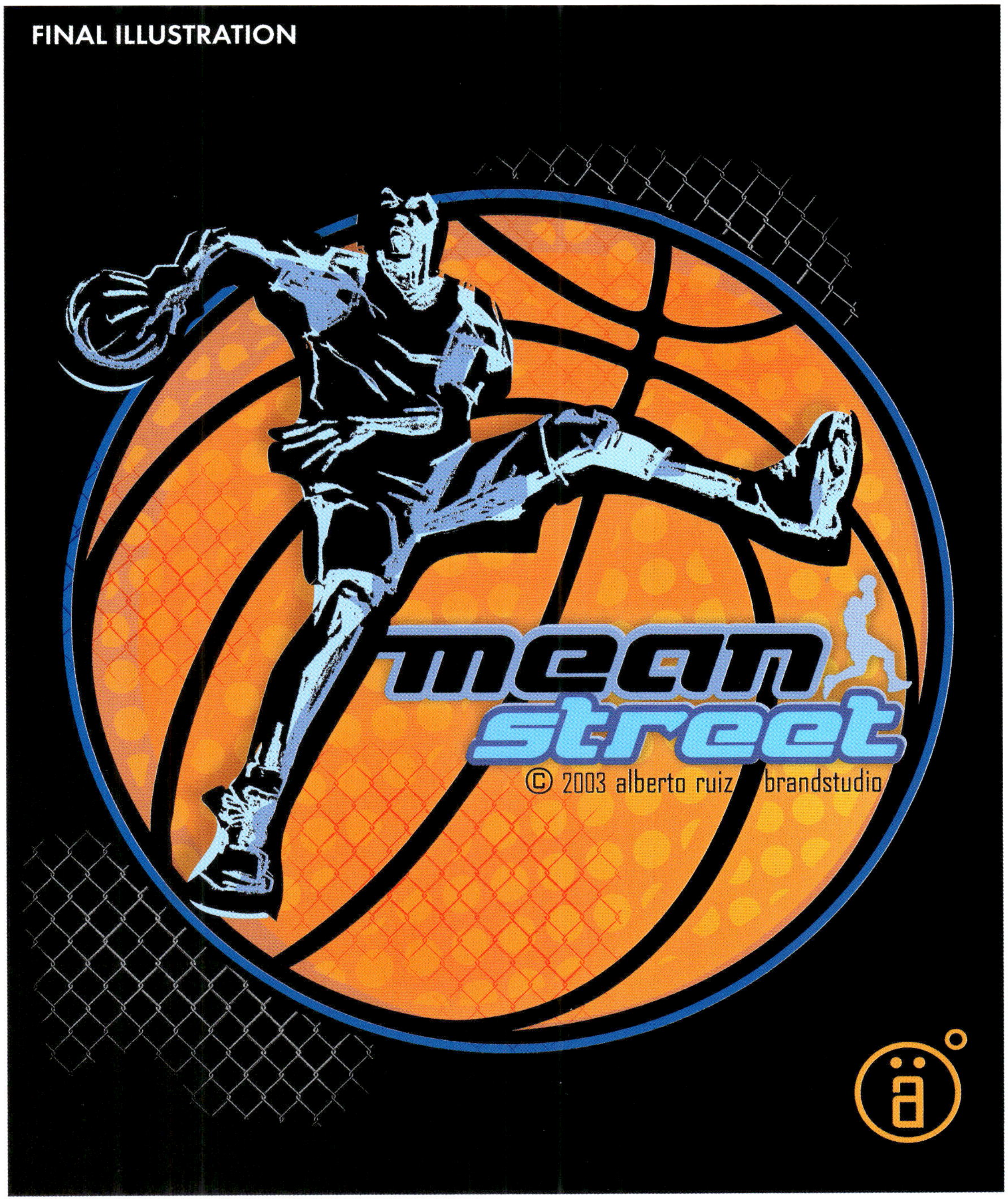

FINAL ILLUSTRATION
mean
street
© 2003 alberto ruiz brandstudio

BLUE JEANS BLUES

Want to give those pants the look and feel of real blue jeans?... I thought you would. Well, all you need is a fabric bitmap, if you don't have one, scan a piece of denim and save it as a TIF bitmap.

I masked the fabric bitmap into the pants' shape by selecting both the bitmap and the pants and choosing Object > Clipping Mask > Make from the top menu bar, you can also use *Command+7 (Mac OS) Ctrl+7 (Windows)* Make sure that the shape is in front of the bitmap you wish to mask. You can color the stroke of any mask, by default the mask has no fill or stroke. The dashed line for the stitching and other details such as buttons were added after the texture was mapped.

TEXTURE BITMAP UNCOLORED

BORING PANTS

COLORED BITMAP

BASE COLOR

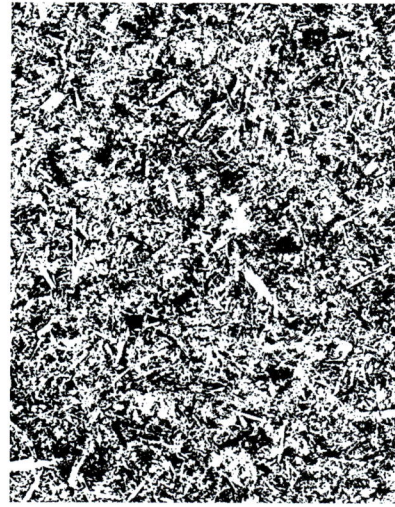

Transparency blend set to multiply at 33% opacity

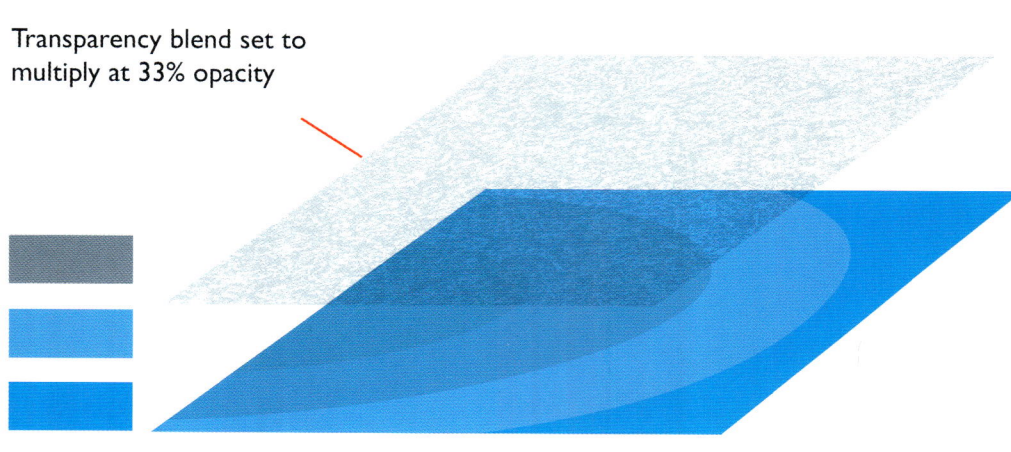

CHIPBOARD BITMAP

BACKGROUND

The entire background was covered with the texture which blended really well with the flat blue circles.

DOT MATRIX DOLL

To create a halftone screen "glow" effect, 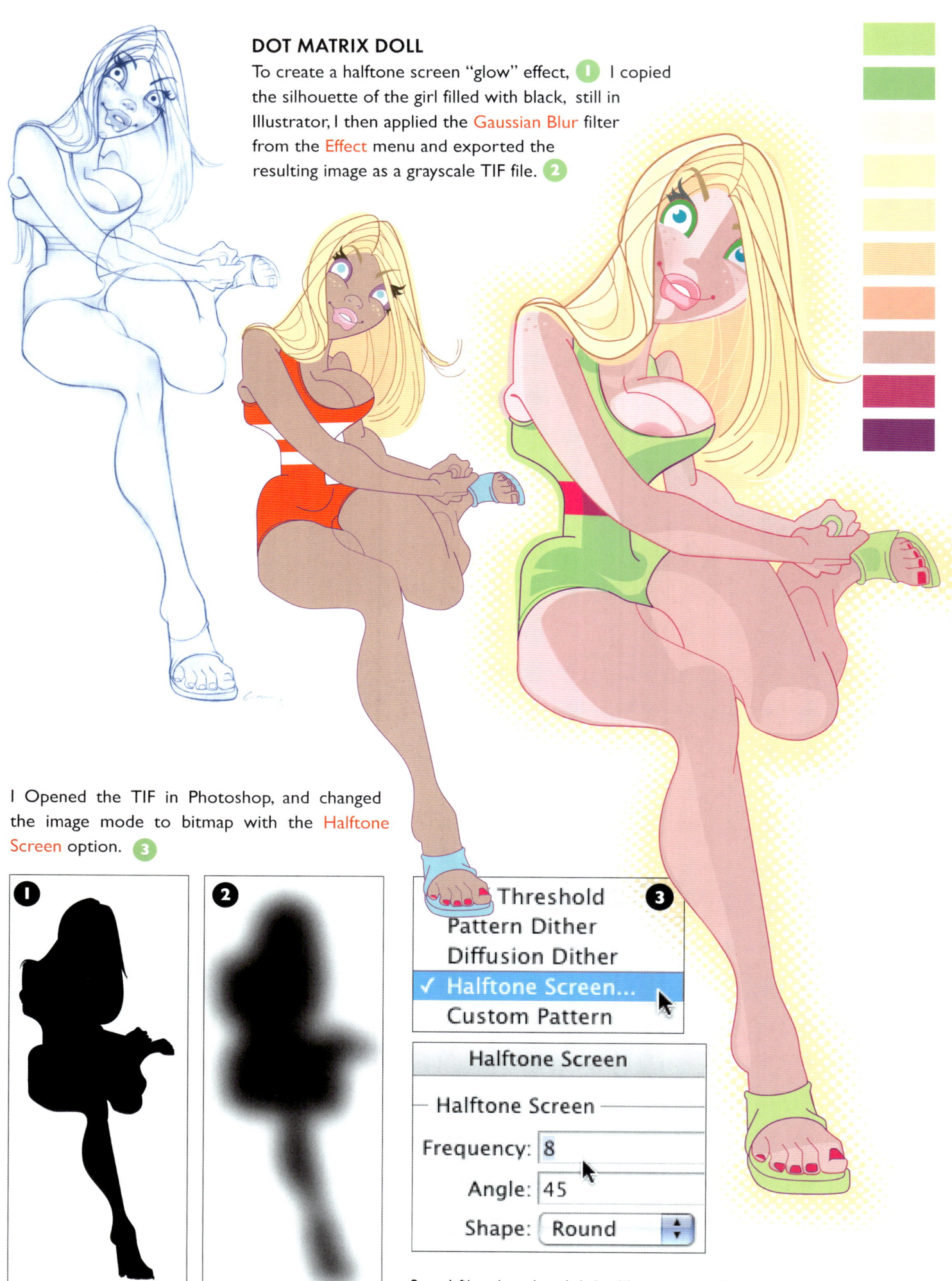 ❶ I copied the silhouette of the girl filled with black, still in Illustrator, I then applied the Gaussian Blur filter from the Effect menu and exported the resulting image as a grayscale TIF file. ❷

I Opened the TIF in Photoshop, and changed the image mode to bitmap with the Halftone Screen option. ❸

❶

❷

❸

Threshold
Pattern Dither
Diffusion Dither
✓ Halftone Screen...
Custom Pattern

Halftone Screen

Halftone Screen

Frequency: 8

Angle: 45

Shape: Round

Saved file, placed in Adobe Illustrator and re-colored.

THE FIRST CARTOON PIN-UP MAGAZINE

BAYSIDE girl ™

JULY/AUG 2008   SAN DIEGO EDITION

4

sketchbook

IN THIS ISSUE

roughs
doodles
sketches
drawings
renderings

PUBLISHED BY | BRAANDSTUDIO PRESS
WWW.BRAANDSTUDIO.COM | NEW YORK CITY

9 44491 90032 9

$15.00 US $25.00 CANADA

recreating a classic deco look

adobe illustrator™

ecreating the look and feel of renaissance decorative art with a digital flair is exactly what Vampirella™ would have wanted. This project was so much fun to do in AI, mainly due to its capabilities to handle text, vector objects as well as a surprisingly robust support for transparency blends, Photoshop users are so jealous.

For this demo , I combined a ssketch, photos, clip art bitmaps, text, rasterized vector images, and more, all without leaving Adobe Illustrator.

I scanned the original red pencil sketch at 450 DPI into Photoshop, I generally use a low resolution TIF or JPG to trace over but this time the sketch won't be used merely as a template, it will actually become part of the finished illustration.

After adjusting the contrast to an acceptable clarity using the Levels slider —command + L (Mac), control + L (Windows) I saved two copies of the scanned art: a high-resolution version (350 DPI) for print, and a lo-res copy (100 DPI) which became my temporary template. I then created a new document in Illustrator and placed the low-resolution file with the Template option checked. The lo-res image would be replaced at the end, for now the 100 DPI image is low enough to keep things moving along at a decent speed.

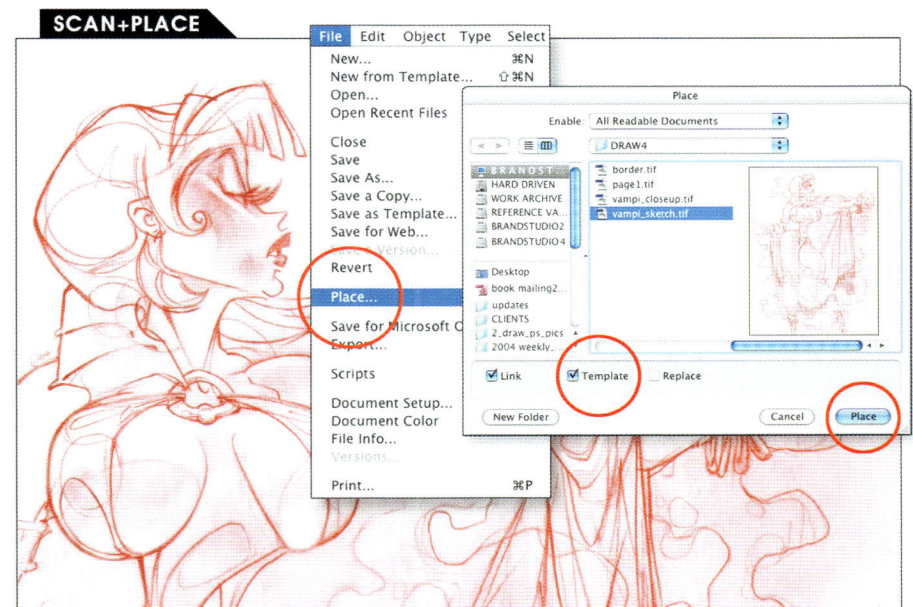

I created a new layer directly above the Template, the logo, background and other complex elements such as the robe were also assigned individual layers.
As usual, I started by "tracing" the main masses with the pen tool, following the "Template" as close as possible. The elements that make up the head were drawn first, the technique used is the same throughout.

Each of the main masses of the body is composed of at least three shapes, layered on top of one another. The first one is a flat-colored skin-tone base, filled with C6 M7 Y10 K0 no stroke (outline) 100 % opaque.

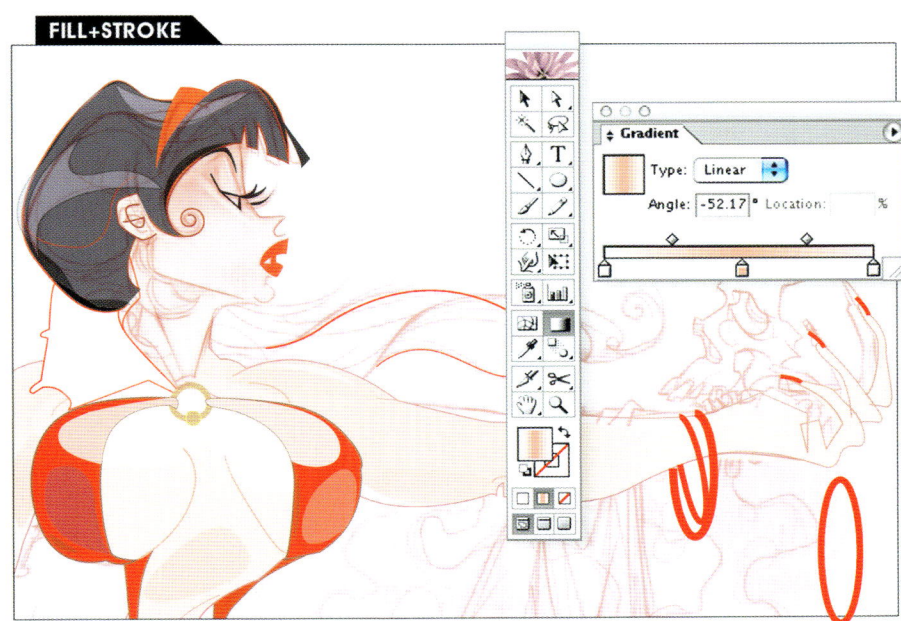

An exact duplicate of this Base Shape is then placed directly on top of the original using the copy and paste-in-front commands —command + C and command + F (Mac), control + C and control + F (Windows). This shape is usually filled with a gradient and a transparency blend, so I'll call it Gradient Shape. The Base Shape is copied once again and pasted in front of the Gradient Shape, this third object has no fill, just a stroke. This I'll name the Outline Shape.

I only used two basic gradients to render the skin (pictured on the right). I call these Cool & Wram Gradients. In order to blend the Gradient Shapes with the Base Shapes in a smooth fashion, I applied one of three transparency modes: Multiply, Color Burn or Color Dodge (these options are found in the 'Transparency Palette'). For more on transparency blends, please see Issue # 8 of Draw! Magazine.

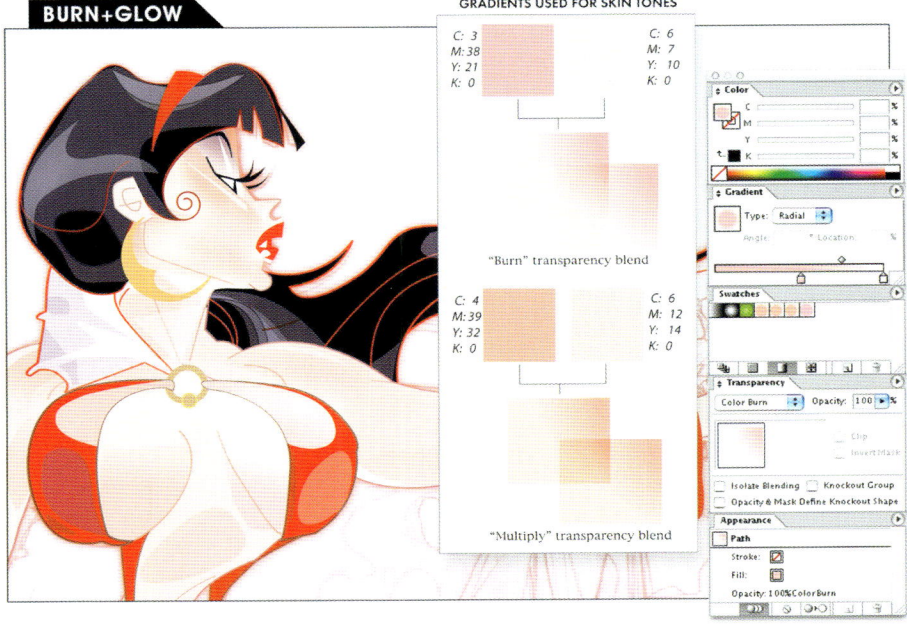

ORIGINAL FONT : "ABADDON" TYPEFACE

1 VAMPIRELLA

2 TYPE CONVERTED TO PATHS: Command/Shift/"O" (Macs), Control/Shift/"O" (Windows)

VAMPIRELLA

3 EDITING INDIVIDUAL LETTERS: Points were deleted and shapes altered with the "Pen" tool.

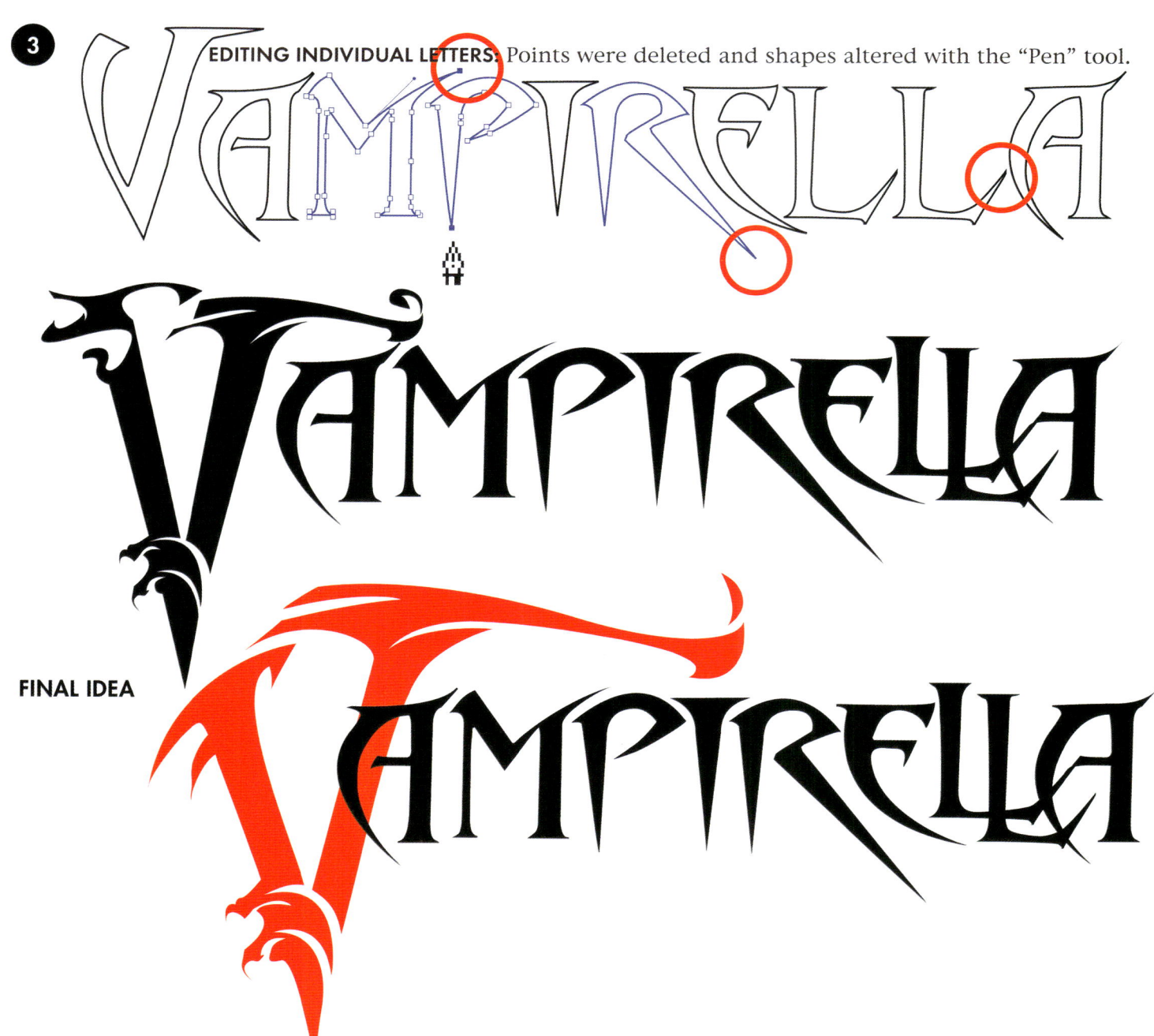

FINAL IDEA

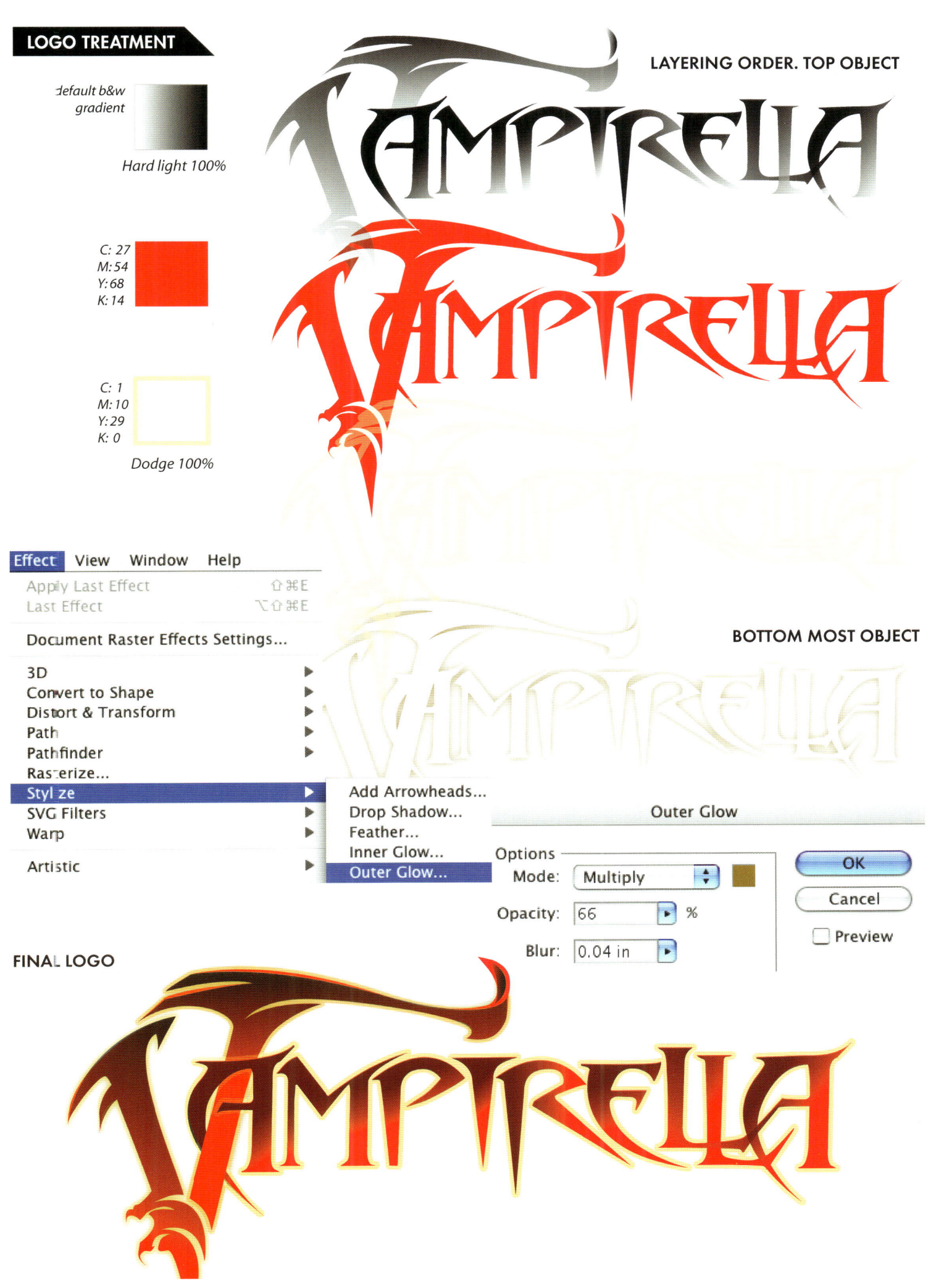

LOGO TREATMENT

default b&w gradient

Hard light 100%

C: 27
M: 54
Y: 68
K: 14

C: 1
M: 10
Y: 29
K: 0

Dodge 100%

LAYERING ORDER. TOP OBJECT

BOTTOM MOST OBJECT

Effect   View   Window   Help

Apply Last Effect   ⇧⌘E
Last Effect   ⌥⇧⌘E

Document Raster Effects Settings...

3D   ▶
Convert to Shape   ▶
Distort & Transform   ▶
Path   ▶
Pathfinder   ▶
Rasterize...
Stylize   ▶
SVG Filters   ▶
Warp   ▶

Artistic   ▶

Add Arrowheads...
Drop Shadow...
Feather...
Inner Glow...
Outer Glow...

Outer Glow

Options
Mode: Multiply
Opacity: 66   %
Blur: 0.04 in

OK
Cancel
☐ Preview

FINAL LOGO

DEFAULT PATTERN COLOR JOB

This pattern is one of the few illustrator repeats that came with the program, I use this one all the time, all I do is re-color it and run a Photoshop filter, BINGO!

1

Click & Drag "SPIRAL" Pattern to document

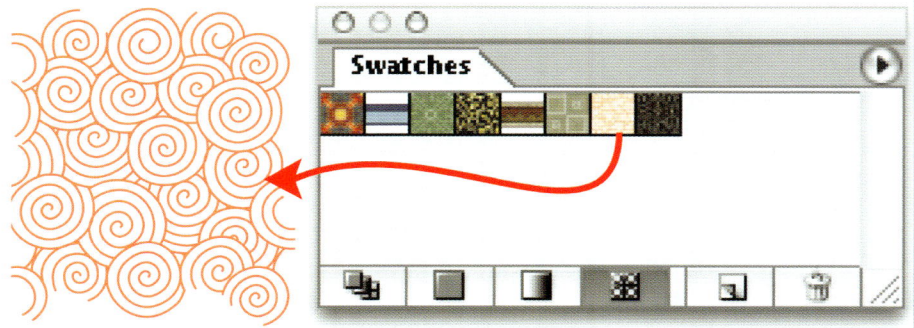

❶ ORIGINAL PATTERN.

2

Click on a path & choose Same">"Stroke Color" from the "Select" menu.

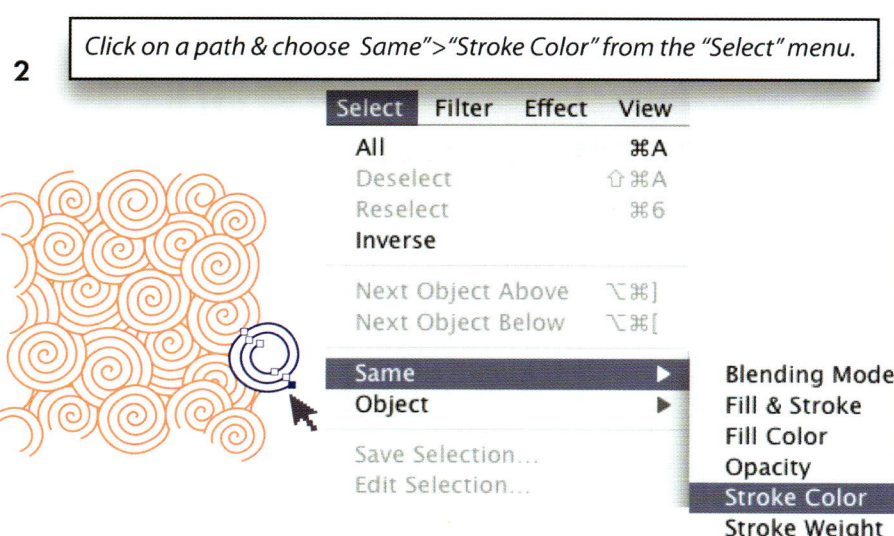

❷ AFTER RE-COLORING.

3

After coloring, select and drag the entire group back to the Swatches box.

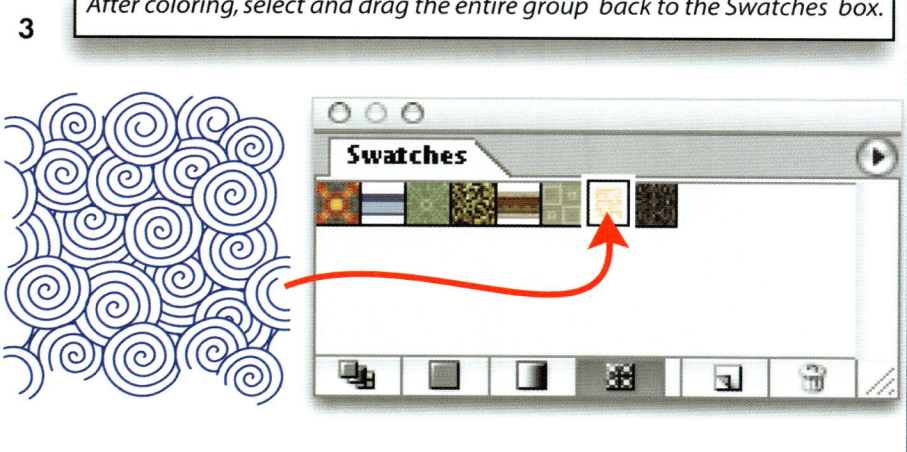

❸ AFTER PS BURN & DODGE

TIP: hold down the "Option" Key while you drop the paths you just re-colored directly on top of the icon representing the pattern you wish to replace, this will automaticaly update all objects filled with the original pattern.

VAMPIRELLA

FRAMING THE IMAGE

I scanned an image drawn by Leonardo DaVinci to use as my backdrop. I edited out parts of the picture using the rubber stamp tool in Photoshop and saved it as a TIF.

① I created a new layer in Illustrator, directly below the Template layer and placed the DaVinci image in it. **②** After changing the red hue to a much brighter orange using the Hue/Saturation control in Photoshop —*command + U (Mac), control + U (Windows)*—

I went back to AI and from the Transparencies palette's pull-down sub menu I selected Multiply and *Voilá!* I exported the file as a TIF at 350 DPI and I was finished. further color hues tweaking was done in Photoshop and the image mode

was changed to CMYK for output. The decorative frame on the right was not used in the final image, but I did explore a couple of background variations with it, actually, a few more than a couple but these are the better ones. (shown below). This image is part of a Dover clip art book called: *Decorative Ornaments And Alphabets Of The Renaissance*

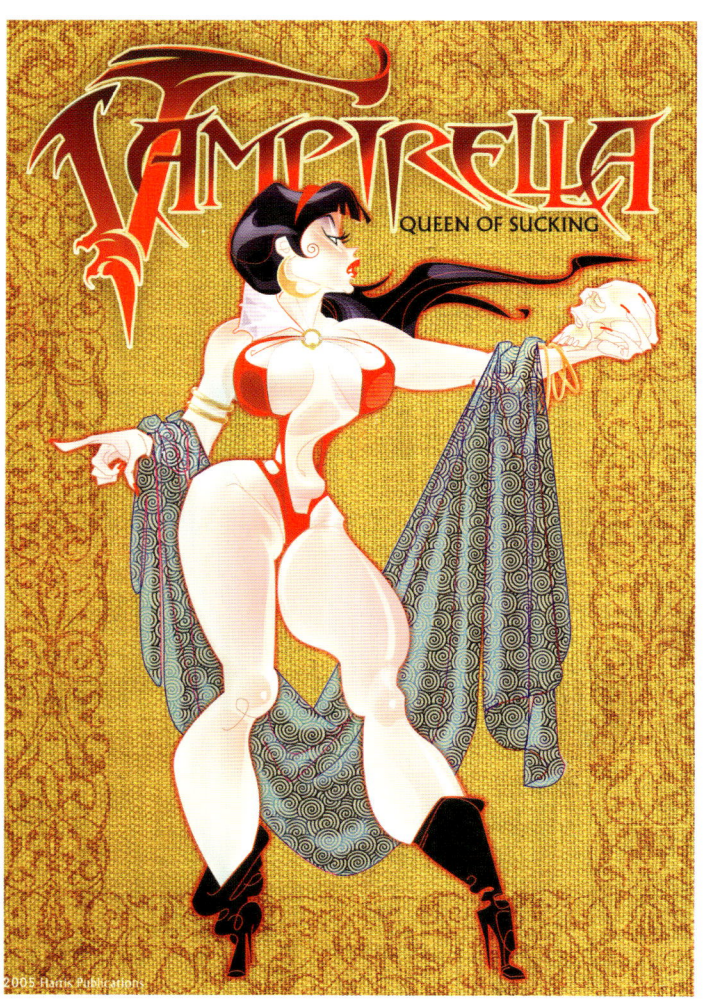

tales of a tiki comic book cover
adobe illustrator™

For this fun assignment I wanted to give the cover the look of the silk-screened posters from the WPA era [Works Progress Administration, 1935 -1943, an arts and information program created by the U. S. government to provide economic relief from the great depression] I went off to experiment with textures, using the symbols palette in Adobe Illustrator. The idea is not to fool the viewer into thinking the end result is an actual painting , but to sort of often the digital feel of a native vector illustration.

The drawing featured on this page was my first idea for the finished cover. I like it a lot but I wanted to use the actual cover assignment to apply the symbols palette goodies built- in Adobe Illustrator CS. I braced myself for a lot of trial and error, since this was my first time using this feature, but to my surprise, the tools and the symbols palette were intuitive and user-friendly.

PREPARING FOR BATTLE

Before I started working in Adobe Illustrator, I put together a comprehensive color sketch in Photoshop. The final image ended up a lot different than the comp (see below) but this was needed to minimize the color and shading guess work, I worked out the color planes, highlights and shadow areas and even the logo placement.

I was bent from the beginning on using an "all-flower" pattern and I carried this idea right towards the end. Eventually I found that it was way too busy to have the girl's dress and the background competing with each other for attention.

Fortunately for me, I had created a few flower repeat patterns for surfer trunks back in my garment district days, so I had a few designs to choose from.

For the sake of this demonstration however and to show you how easy it really is to generate a pattern in Illustrator, I re-drew and put together a new "tossed" flower repeat based on the old designs.

THE USUAL, PLEASE

As with most of my illustrations involving preliminary drawings, I scanned the original pencil rough at 150 DPI and saved the image in TIF format so I can then use as a template. After creating a new document in AI I placed the file by choosing Place from the File menu with the Template option checked.

I then locked the current layer (Layer 1 or template) created a second layer which I re-named "coloring" and dragged directly underneath. This is the layer in which I'll be doing most of the work, I used just one layer for this illustration, quite a departure from the 20 plus layer gargantuan files I normally deal with.

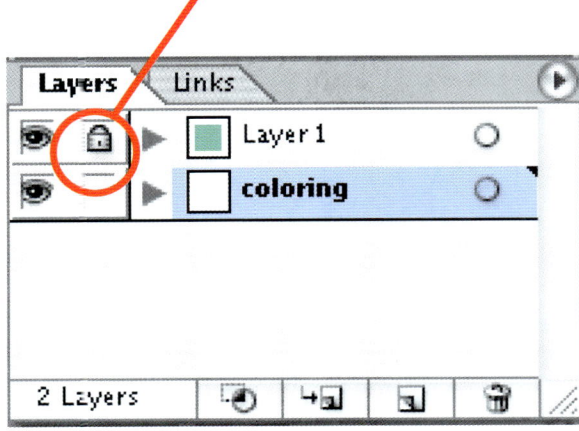

CREATING A PATTERN

I scanned these in Photoshop, at screen resolution (72 DPI), placed them in Illustrator and proceeded to trace over them with the pen tool, black stroke/black fill white background .

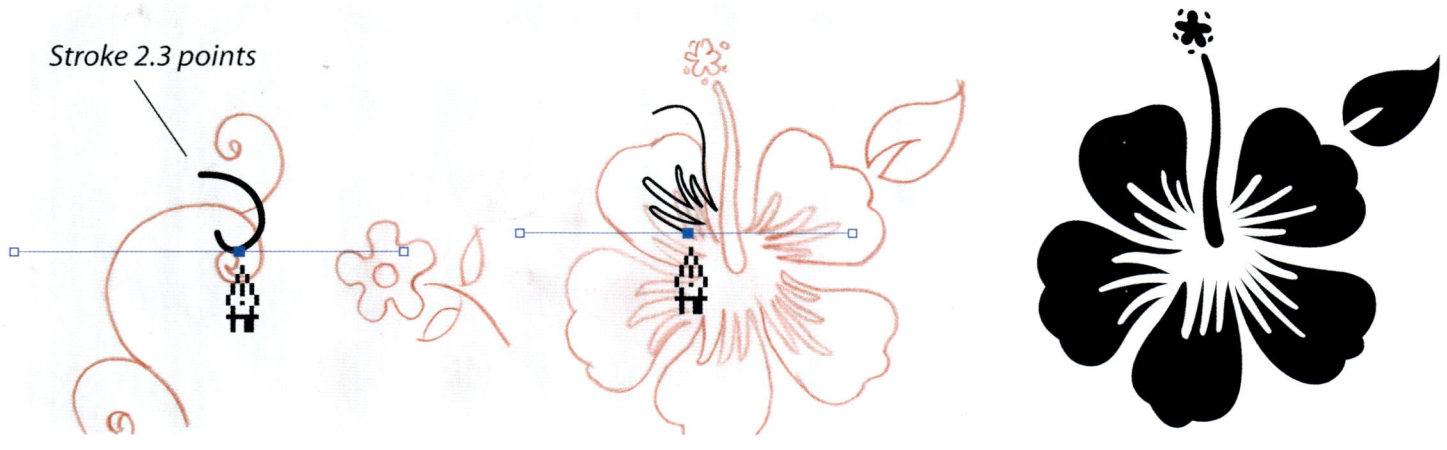

Stroke 2.3 points

The same 3 sets of elements were copied several times, flipped, rotated and scaled at random. A black background color was added and the color of the flowers inversed

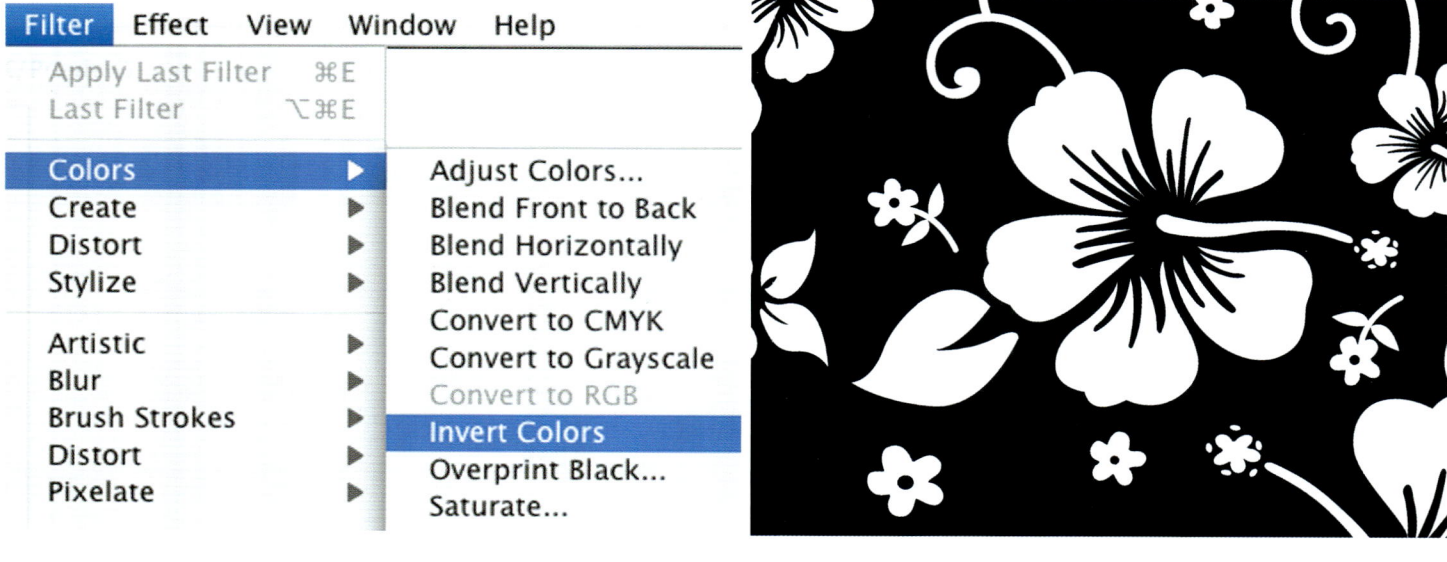

FINAL PATTERN.

Once I was done moving and scaling the objects to my satisfaction, I dragged the resulting mess into the swatches palette.

After the b & w pattern was created, I generated a few more color ways based on my color ideas for the overall illustration. For a quick tip on how to re-color patterns check out DRAW! Magazine #10.

SHAPE SHIFTER

Using the pen tool, I traced over my sketch, blocking out the main shapes, as usual, working from back to front. The hand with the gun was drawn separately and pasted in back of the girl.
Both the top and skirt were filled with one of the previously created patterns, the pattern itself was modified to conform to the girl's curvaceous back side (see below)

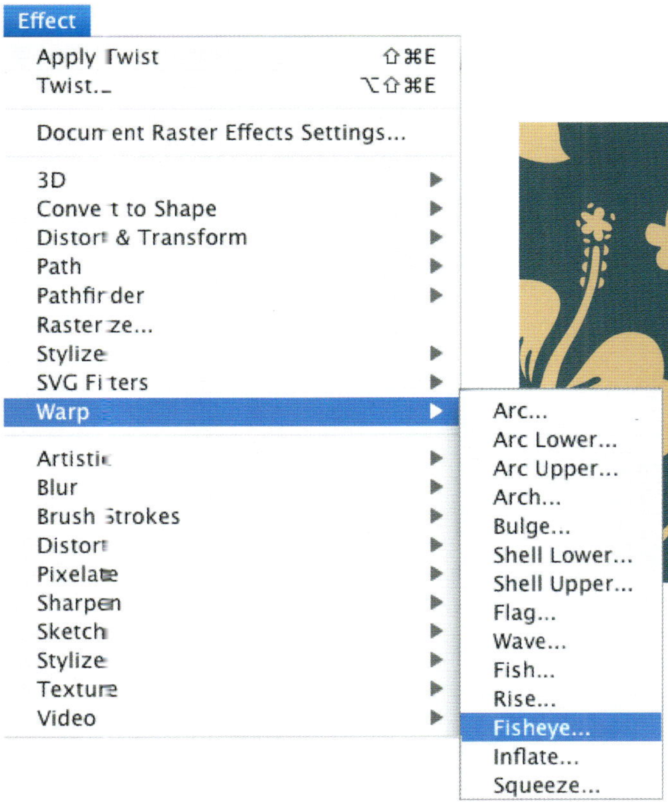

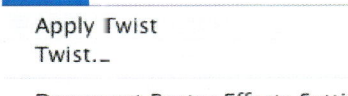

Normal

WARP SPEED

Rather than to re-draw some of the elements of the pattern fo follow the girls' contour, I applied the "Fisheye" effect to the mask containing the skirt flower design.

After Warp>Fisheye Effect

SEXY SYMBOLS

Symbols turned out to be a lot of fun to work with, I haven't been too thrilled with them in the past, too predictable and stiff for my taste. Adobe Illustrator has improved on this old concept, it sports a nice set of tools to help you harness those pesky vector freaks, although I must say they require a lot of RAM to function properly, in a slower machine they take forever to re-draw on the screen.

The tools themselves can become sluggish at times but overall, symbols can be very useful and fun to experiment with.

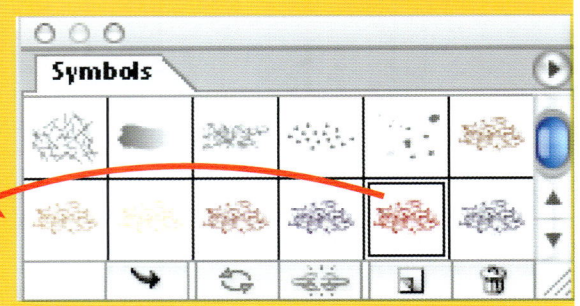

Click & Drag symbol to artboard, re-color and drag back into symbol's palette. Then apply symbol using the spray can tool, it's that easy!

For this illustration I used only one symbol, "Mezzotint", you can find it following this path: "WINDOW">Symbol Libraries>"Artistic Texture".

NOTE: You must expand the symbol after you drag it out of the palette, by selecting expand (from the "OBJECT" menu) in order to modify it.

I researched night and day looking for a decent tiki to draw not knowing I had in my possession the "Native Art" collection of clip images from House Industries, what a time saver!.

These came in handy for sure, just the right touch for the logo portion of the main header.

I wanted a more menacing looking tiki idol than the one provided so I messed around a bit to achieve the "terror" I was looking for.

These designs as well all of the main title fonts used for these project are part of the "Native Art" collection available from House Industries House Industries, P.O. Box 30000, Wilmington, DE 19805.

LOGO TREATMENTS

tales of a tiki cover

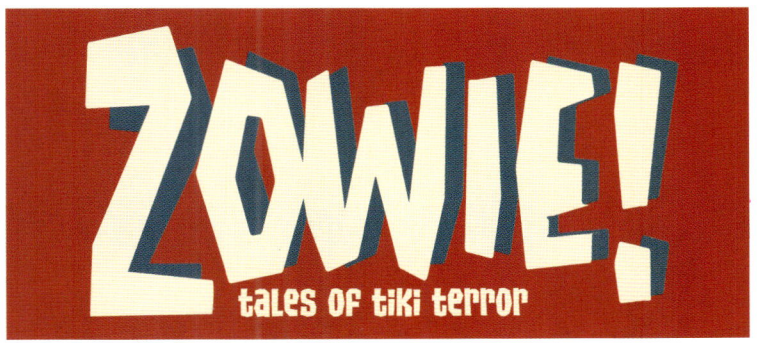

tales of tiki terror

tales of tiki terror

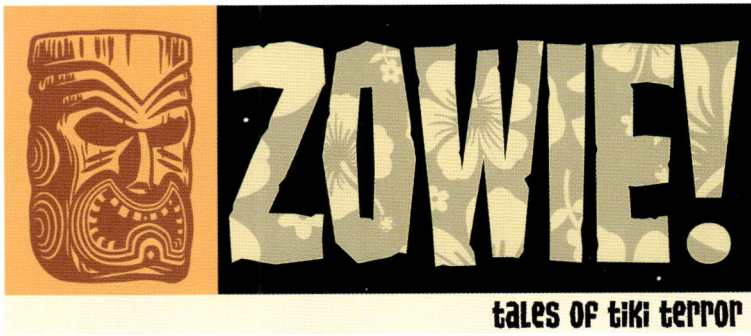

tales of tiki terror

tales of tiki terror

THE EFFECTS OF TRANSPARENCY BLENDING

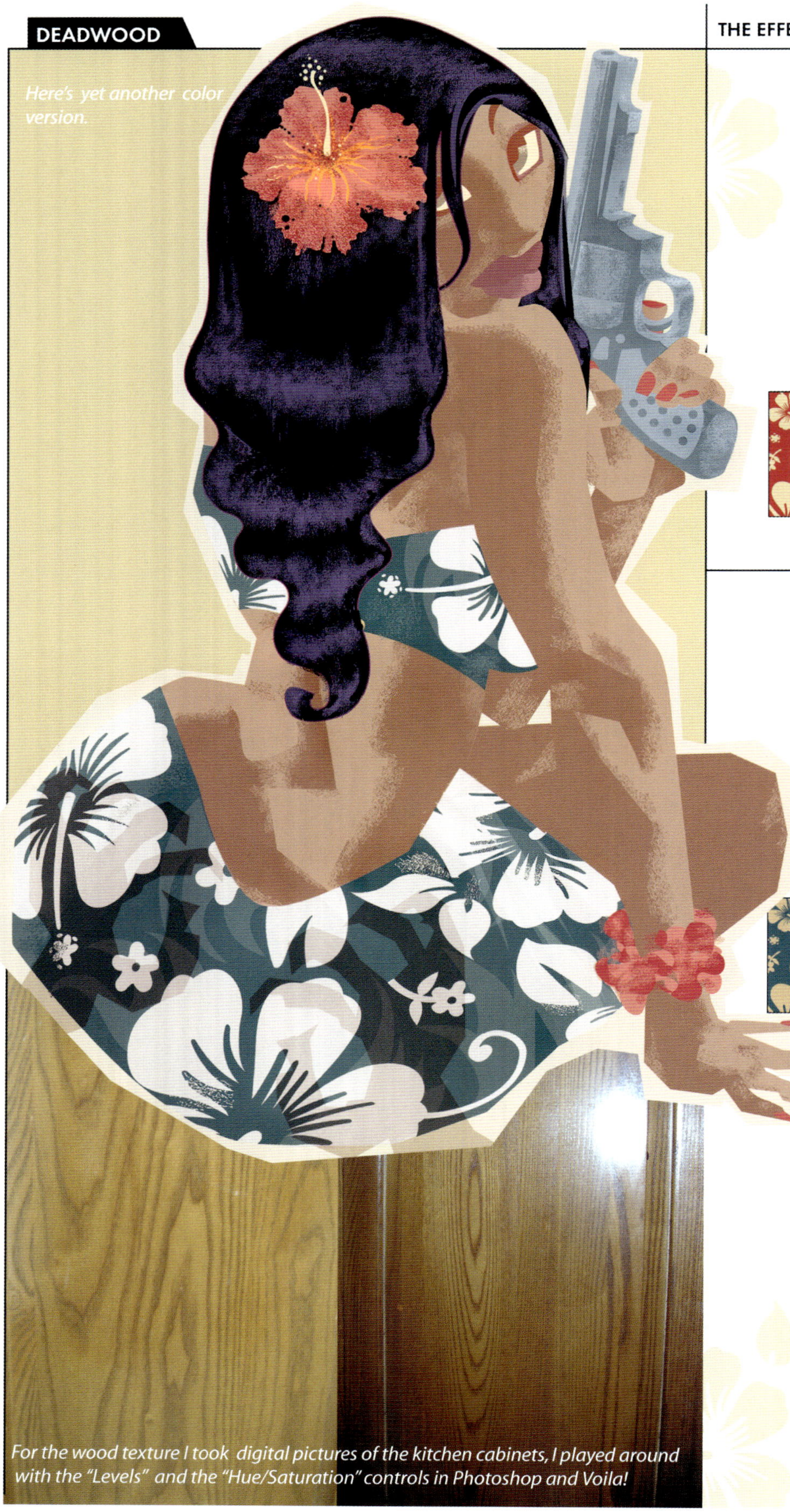

Here's yet another color version.

Wood Panel Blended With Red Pattern

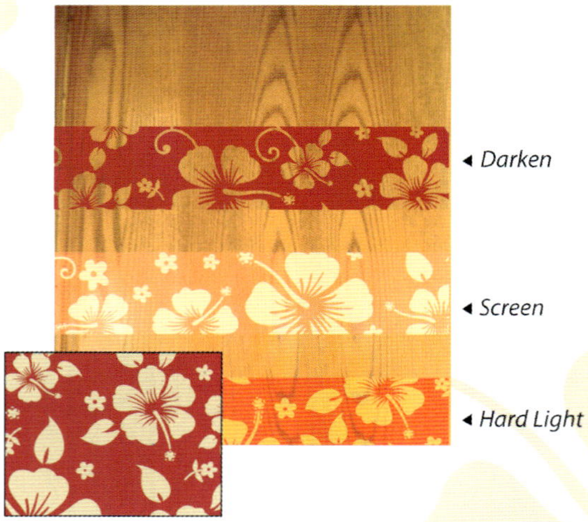

◄ *Darken*

◄ *Screen*

◄ *Hard Light*

Wood Panel Blended With Green Pattern

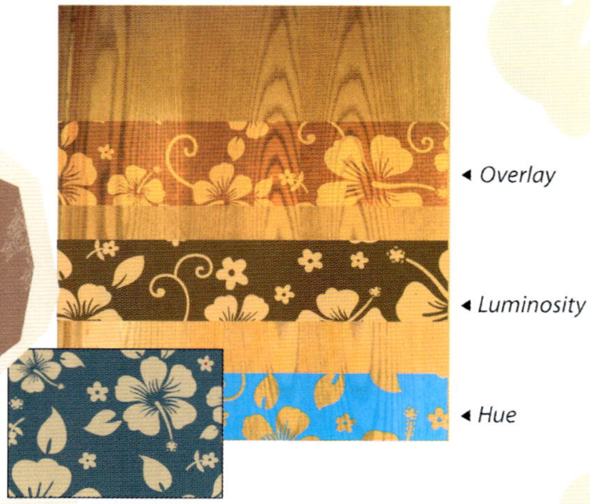

◄ *Overlay*

◄ *Luminosity*

◄ *Hue*

Green Pattern Set At "Soft Light"

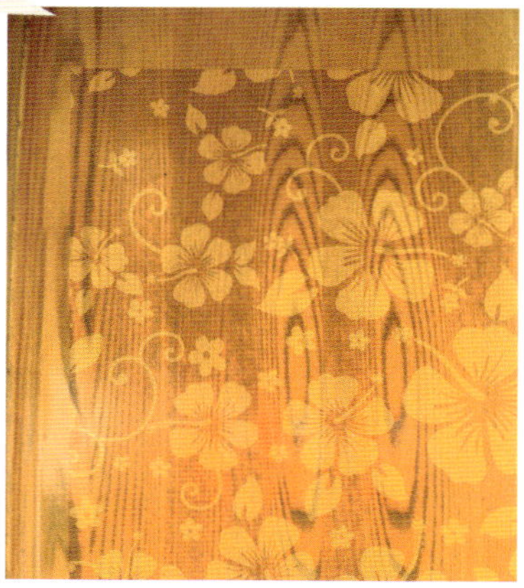

For the wood texture I took digital pictures of the kitchen cabinets, I played around with the "Levels" and the "Hue/Saturation" controls in Photoshop and Voila!

deadline hunter
adobe illustrator™

The deadline for the new Draw! Magazine article was fast approaching. and instead of choosing a random Adobe Illustrator tool to write about, I decided to use the current sketchbook cover I was working on, to illustrate a typical "tight deadline" assignment.

The final cover Illustration took one day to complete; the article, well, that's another story. The concept was based on an unused preliminary sketch I never got the chance to use. Salsipuedes is the name of a famous hanging bridge in the almost inaccessible mountains of Ecuador. I've always thought the name was interesting and fitting, because in Spanish "Sal si puedes" means "get out if you can" which is precisely what one thinks while crossing the bridge.

As it turns out the peculiar moniker is not as original as I once believed. An internet search resulted in more than two dozen towns throughout the Americas and Spain bearing the same name, including a California municipality and school district.

The concept plays on the literal meaning of the set of words that make up the name. Because I was both, the client and the art director for this assignment, the approval process was a snap! I showed the preliminary rough to Alberto (my art director and account manager) and he approved it with but a few minor changes, he then showed the concept to the client (Mr. A. Ruiz) who was delighted with the clever concept and stamped his seal of approval on the spot.

PLEASE RECYCLE

Through the years, I've managed to keep a pretty substantial amount of preliminary, unused and unfinished repeat patterns, I either created or converted for use in the garment industry. This effort has paid good dividends, time and time again..

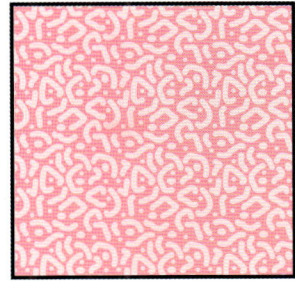

THINKING IN SHAPES

As with most of the work colored in Illustrator, I started by drawing the main shapes with the Pen tool, following the pencil line as close as possible and simplifying complex shapes as I went along.

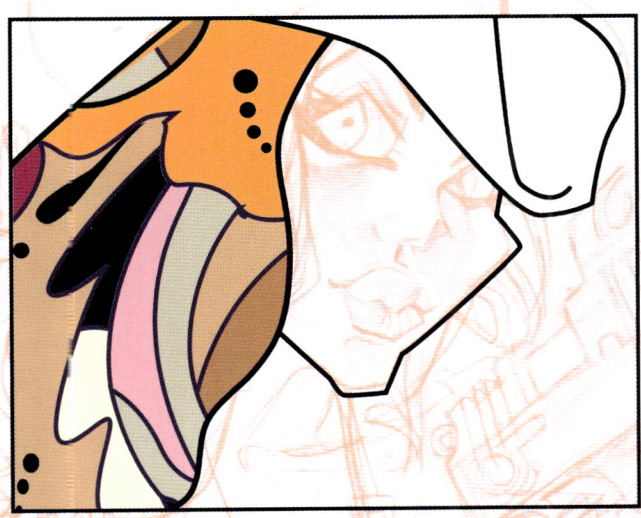

All the shapes conforming the face and body were filled with the same (pink to white) gradient, using the white of the paper as both mid-tone and high-light color, good opportunitty to apply "negative shape" theories. There is no time for excessive detail such as hair and other complicated minutiae. I filled in the two hair shapes with an old,

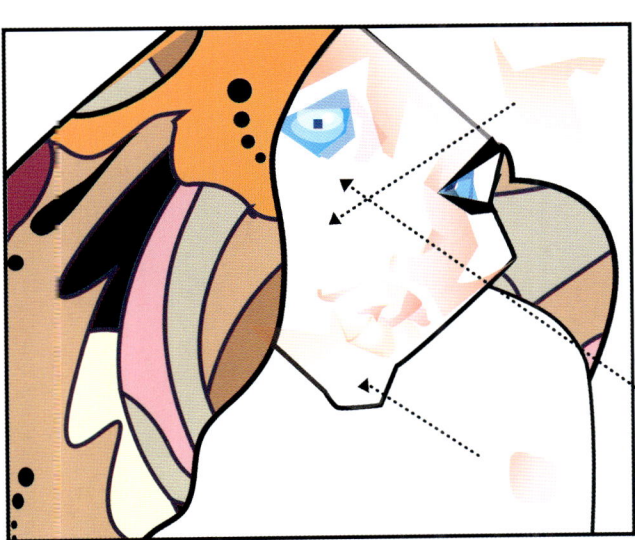

unused abstract flower repeat pattern I had created a zillion years ago for textile use, I used a more "populated" pattern for the cowboy hat, in direct contrast with the broader, flatter shapes of the hair fill.

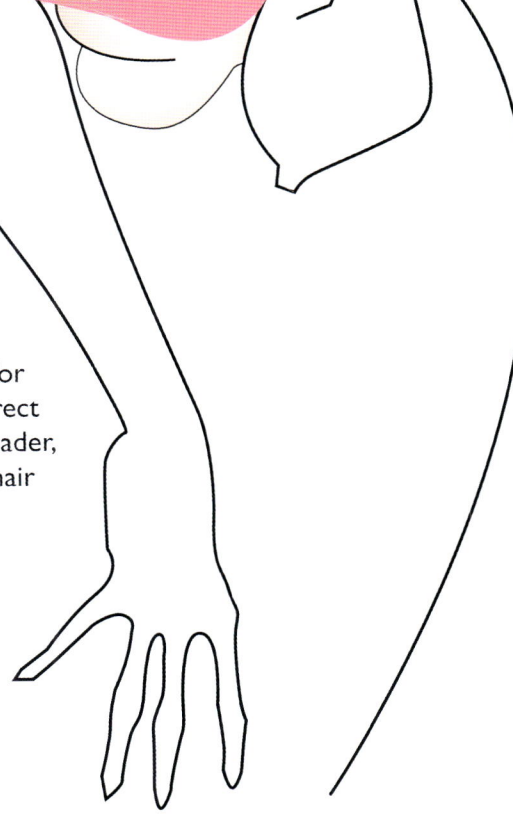

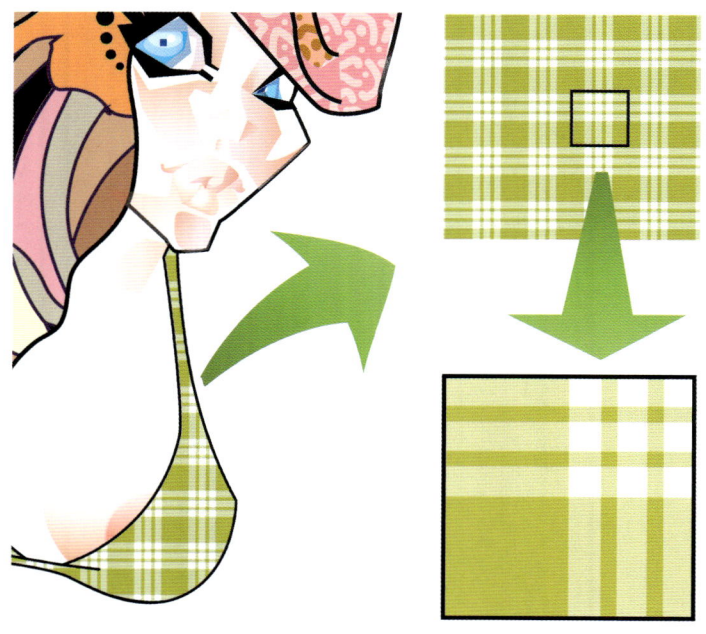

Quick Color Ways

If you use tints of the same custom color, one click is all you need to switch colors (you must select the entire repeat).

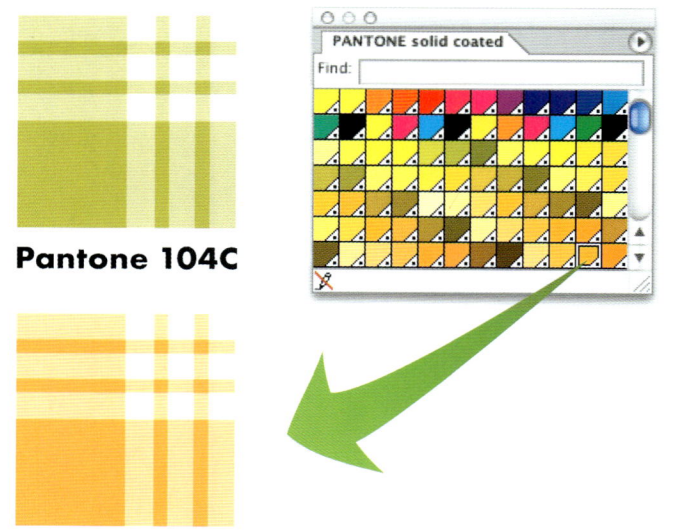

Pantone 104C

Pantone 143C

Pantone 104C

Using the Rectangle tool, I drew the horizontal shapes and fill them in with a custom color.

1

Pantone 104C 50%

The vertical shapes came next, I used a tint of the same color.

2

If you use CMYK or RGB colors, you can always switch colors via the Adjust Colors module found in the Filter menu, on the top menu bar.

Divide & Conquer **3**

Selected all the shapes and applied the Divide filter.

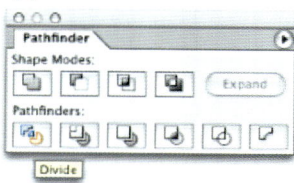

Clean Up

I discarded the unwanted shapes outside of our repeat rectangle, re-colored the shapes, placed a white rectangle in the back and drag the newly created pattern into the swatches box.

4

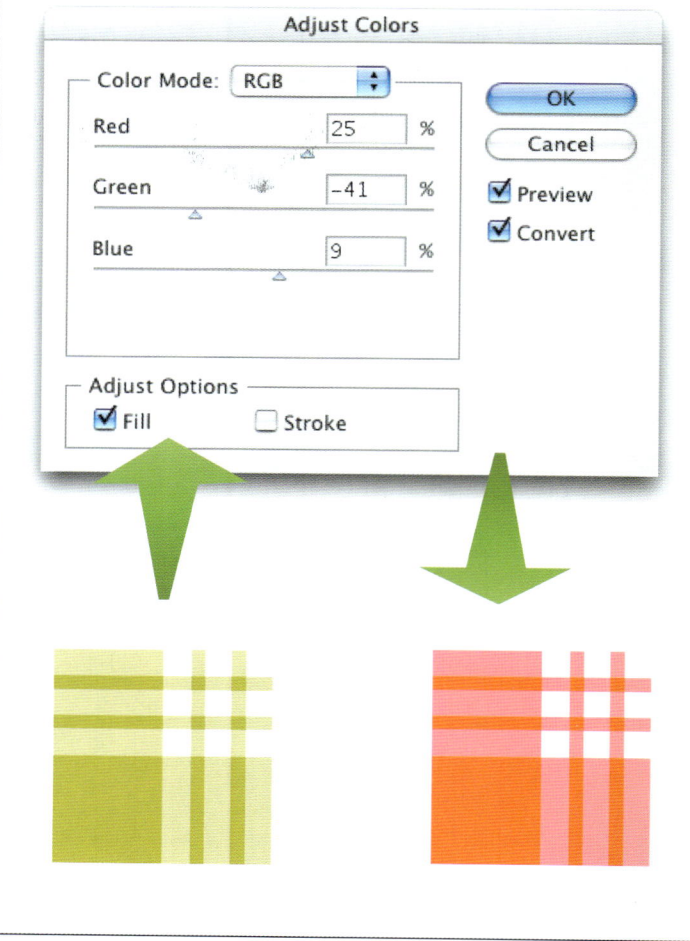

BUILD YOUR OWN FAKE RAY GUN
LAYERING SEQUENCE

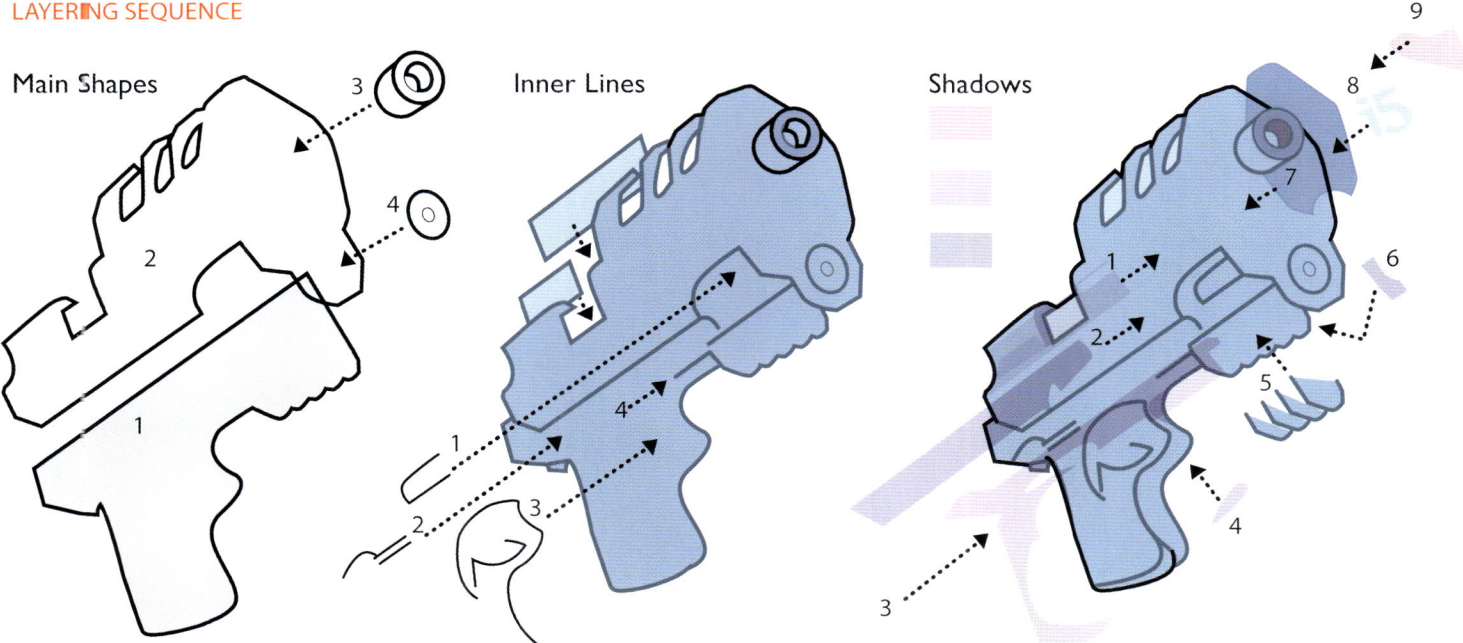

Main Shapes

Inner Lines

Shadows

To make it easy to just drop color inside the gun, I drew 2 outlines and filled the shapes with the inner lines afterwards.

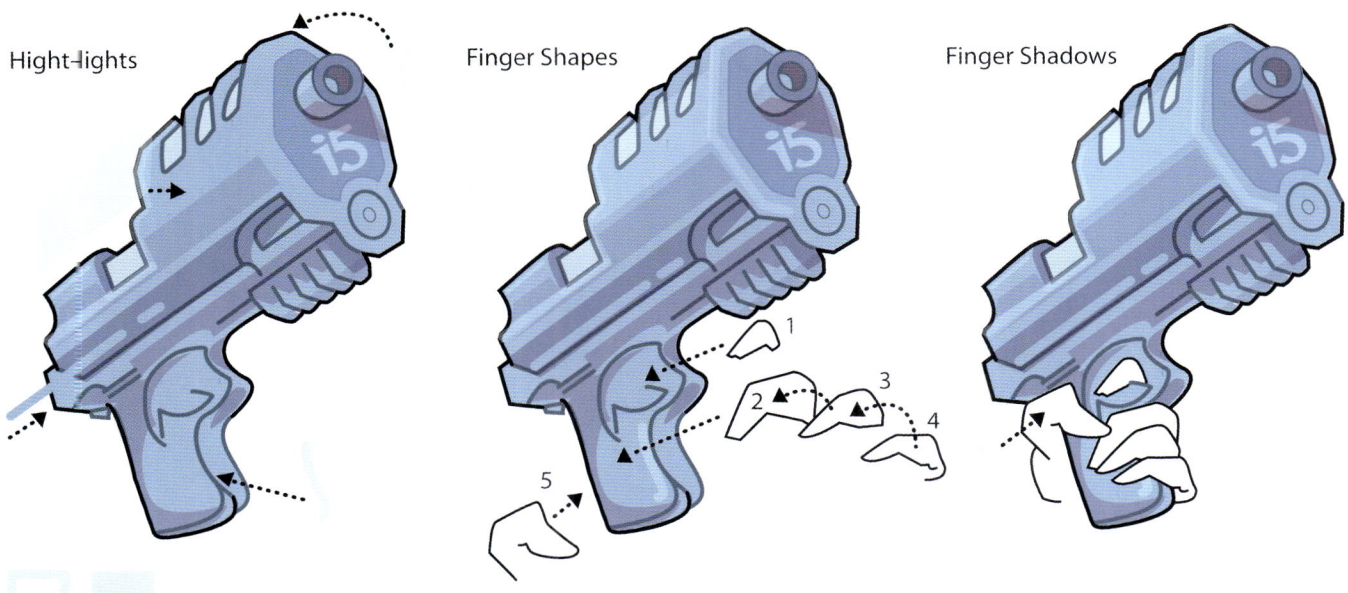

Hight-lights

Finger Shapes

Finger Shadows

More than to show the process , I did this because it was a lot of fun. I'm not showing you anything you haven't seen before. I just love diagrams and schematics, I know you do too.

Finger Nails

THE PUMP DON'T WORK 'CAUSE THE VANDALS TOOK THE HANDLE*

As usual, I layered my shapes overlapping from back to front, setting the transparency blends to Darken or Multiply for shadows and Screen or Color Dodge for the high-lights .

The bumps under the barrell of the gun project a shadow that is contrary to the light source. I drew half of one of the shapes and the open path looked kind of neat, I dragged the first shape while holding down the Option key *(Alt in Windows)* and then hit *command+D (control+D)* three times. They may be inaccurate but they lend "texture" to an otherwise flat object so I left them alone. Please don't email me to tell me the gun is not realistic, who's gonna know?

SALSIPUEDES ¡5!

Main font used: Emulate Seriff from the "T26" collection of typefaces http://www.t26.com/fonts.php

1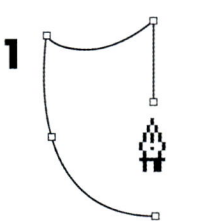

CUTTING IT CLOSE

Using the Pen tool I drew one half of the shield shape.

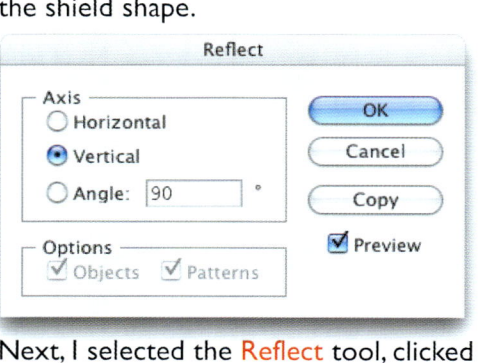

2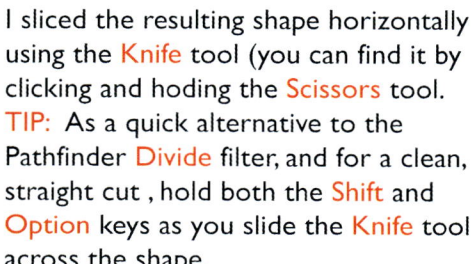

Next, I selected the Reflect tool, clicked on the vertical axis button, typed '90' in the Angle field (for a 90 degree flip) and clicked on the Copy button. I then merged both halves using the Pathfinder Add to shape area tool.

3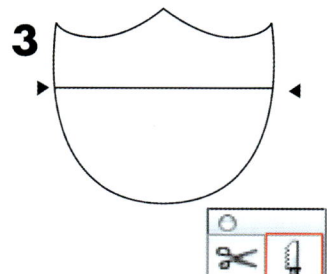

I sliced the resulting shape horizontally using the Knife tool (you can find it by clicking and hoding the Scissors tool. TIP: As a quick alternative to the Pathfinder Divide filter, and for a clean, straight cut , hold both the Shift and Option keys as you slide the Knife tool across the shape.

I colored the individual shapes and added the type.

4

sketchbook

Font: Bureau Agency regular.

MAP IT!

An old map of the area was added to the background to drive home the point. A green square was drawn over the map and its transparency blend was set to Multiply.

To soften the map, I applied the Blur filter from the Effects menu.

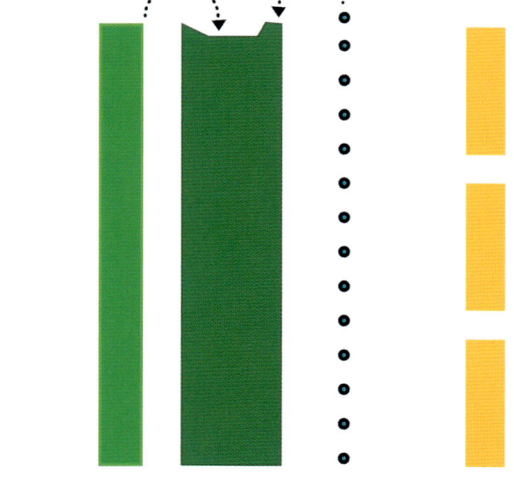

LINE WEIGHTS

The pole consists of two lines: the dark green base is 38 points thick and the light green Hight-light stroke is 15 points. The dotted yellow lines are also 15 points heavy.

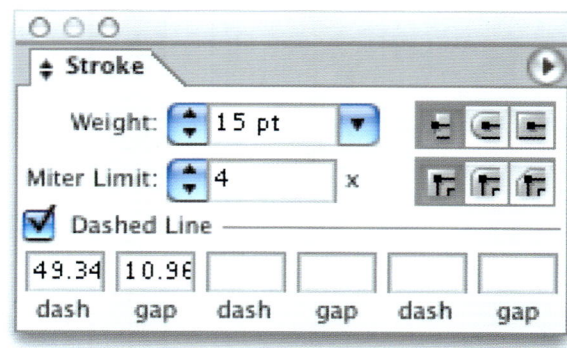

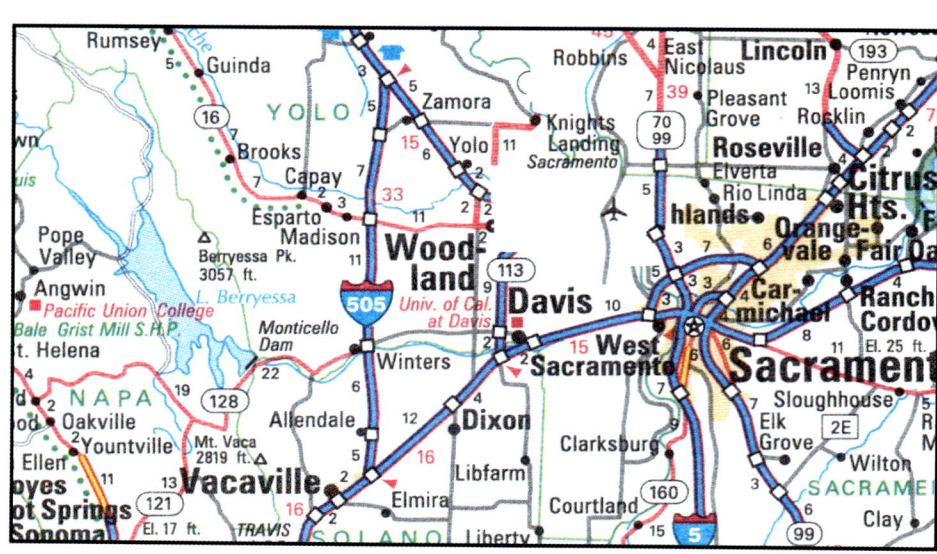

deadline hunter

for more on Alberto Ruiz and his work,
please visit
processjunkie.blogspot.com
send your emails to:
alberto@brandstudio.com

To order additional copies of this book and to
view our catalog of titles currently in print,
please visit:
www.brandstudiopress.com

For volume purchases and resale inquiries please contact us at:
booksales@brandstudio.com

special thanks to Mike Manley at Draw! Magazine and Eric Nolen Weathington at TwoMorrows.